Dedication

I dedicate this book to my beloved wife Carolina, whose presence in my life for the last eleven years has brought the gifts of spirit and harmony, companionship and unity to my personal life and mission, and without whom the joy of our three children — Alexandra, Charles and David-Gabriel — would have never been realized as manifestations of heaven on earth.

I honor the memory of my parents, who, from the dimensions where they watch over us here, are a continuing reenactment of their deep lessons for real living.

And to you, the reader, who has found your way to these pages, may our date in spirit be fulfilled now that we have met in the deep sense of our Mission.

Contents

The Soul Remembers

A Parable on Spiritual Transformation

Carlos Warter, M.D.

Cover art by
Douglas Taylor

ISBN 0-929385-36-5

Published by
Light Technology Publishing
P.O. Box 1526
Sedona, AZ 86339

Printed by
MISSION POSSIBLE
COMMERCIAL PRINTING
P.O. Box 1495
Sedona, AZ 86339

Introduction

I would like you to journey with me on a parable of discovery. We will explore an area of existence where the rules of everyday life do not apply. The rules that keep the dimensions separate limit our ability to comprehend that we are really multidimensional beings operating in different levels of reality and comprehending the space/time continuum according to these rules. Each level of the parable is a metaphor for our life, our culture and the stage our civilization is experiencing.

The conditioning toward fragmentation within the old paradigm has induced a fiction in our world that we have collectively agreed to participate in. As a result of the cages in which we have lived, more than once we have reached a point where we have doubted that the human race would survive. Massive problems have brought us to the brink many times even in the last century. But we have always survived.

The invisible hand of destiny has always been there to turn our individual, social and planetary lives toward the next step of conscious evolution, thus transforming what seemed a global crisis to a lesson in survival. This has been happening even more in the inner realms of human consciousness, because the energy of crisis seems to accelerate the understanding of our essential nature at deep levels.

There is a vibration that rises above the cages of our conditioning from underlying spiritual frequencies that guide us toward our highest good. It is a silvery light we trust, quite pure and intense, but there is another, higher light — love — which brings a strength and warmth that makes all the difference. We evoke this light as the guiding force in this adventure which I invite you to join.

The golden warmth will enable the reader to follow this book on three levels. Each prayer can be heard, and granted, by the higher forces if said thrice: First, for the well-being of our ancestry and lineage; second, for our fellow man; and third, for our own well-being.

As you embark on this reading adventure, read this book three times also. First, from inside the cage of cultural conditioning; second, as if reading it to a listener in the hallway; and third, diving into the essence of what is written and just being there.

As we emerge into a global civilization in which humanity's identity shifts from regional to universal, each individual begins to see himself as an essence and to expand to a multidimensional perspective, savoring the miracle of being alive.

This leads us to an awareness that we no longer need to play death games to understand eternal life. We need no longer process every incident and focus on eliminating the negative, but can instead activate an expansion of consciousness toward full identification with our cosmic individuality.

Our human form and functions, relationships and roles, genetic makeup and background, have long disguised the majesty of our spirits. We are being repositioned to become transducing/receiving devices for cosmic information that expands our awareness of the divine Mission throughout different planets, galaxies and universes coexisting in parallel realities.

Readers in different countries have reported that this book, when read as instructed, has played a powerful role in their own spiritual transformation. This material is intended to reach levels of consciousness where shifts in self-identity can take place and DNA codes can become activated, opening the doorway to the memory of, and identification with, the vaster history of life.

We dare hope that it becomes one of the many spirit-generated tools that are now freeing individuals from limited consciousness and external authority, which have disempowered humanity for ages. We dare hope that it will trigger the soul awareness and the vision of heaven on earth that is genetically lodged in every cell of every physical being so that it may be cocreated by all.

In this journey the most profound adventure is that of rediscovering the sacred, which is who we are. The oneness inspired by the larger Mission statement is the universal consciousness that now shares the gifts of the Creator with you, beloved reader and fellow traveler on this path.

Now is the time for the elevation of matter and the descent of spirit through the cyberspiritual net of the heart, ignoring appearance, race, creed, color, gender, circumstance or even origin.

It is in this divine essence that we meet and rearrange our destiny throughout the worlds we transit with the Almighty's divine love.

Carlos Warter, M.D.
Sedona, Spring 1996

Prologue

We are here at last — at the climax of many cycle-endings. The histories of many, many cooperating planets, systems and dimensions — and the accompanying realizations/wisdoms — have now rearranged space-time. We have experienced a time collapse, a reorganization of history, a transcendence within the dimensional split and a leap up to the next spiral of these coinciding cycles — the next initiation. We have forged a new connection between physical-mass consciousness and consciousness of the All, between love at the cellular level and Love at the Creator level.

I sit in the garden of Light with my ascended family — my wife Bhakti-Shadai and our son Eliyanand and daughter Aeterna. The smell of nectar of the Mystic Purple Rose fills the ethers as we expand our consciousness to encompass it.

This is, once again, Tria Ra. But not the physical, third-dimensional planet — that went the way of earth/Terra. This is *etheric*, fifth-dimensional Tria Ra, and from here we can see it all.

We can see our planet's denser twin spinning in space, emptied of all but a few hardy (that is, *almost* Self-remembering) survivors. These now call out to us for guidance, not yet realizing that in the multidimensional awareness we are one Spirit organizing all levels of density according to individuated pictures of Reality.

We can also see all earths simultaneously: the ancient civilizations (Atlantis, Lemuria, Amazonia, Rome, Greece, Egypt still there, still operating); the earth-that-was up to the last moment (the beautiful green forests; the blue roaring ocean; the plundered core and surface; the struggle for power between the great powers and the haves and the have-nots; the twilight masters fighting for control and domination; humanity reduced to automatons in their amnesia); and the Earth-that-is-no-more, only a few rocks tumbling without purpose through the universe, bearing a few hardy, bodiless survivors.

We can see the stars and beyond — through time and beyond, space and beyond.

My son, now suckled tenderly in your mother's arms, although you cannot yet speak in words, your thoughts and those of your sister are of course clear to me. Now you ripple forth a question, which permeates my etheric robe. You want to know your lineage — from whence you came — and how all that occurred came to pass. I will tell you both gladly.

Let us go, then, on a little journey through memory. (Now I manifest my silver transtime-space-energy-matter vehicle. Bhakti-Shadai enters the vehicle, the children in her arms; she sits and, aligned with the purpose of the Mission, calmly waits.)

My children, this is not a story to be heard only with the ears or for entertainment of the eyes (although it certainly is that, too). This is a story to be lived — to be passionately multiexperienced. It is strange, yes, and multileveled, yes — but you have it in your Soul genes to understand it.

All divine Beings can access the key to their DNA, which, as you will comprehend, was dysfunctional on earth for long periods of creation. Thus memory was restricted there to events in the material plane. Cosmic memory, when awakened, redesigns history.

You are about to multiexperience the story of you — and of the heritage of Being.

We have co-created these events, and for this gift of creativity we are grateful. For it is by the Grace of God that we are able to be in full alignment with Source.

Bhakti-Shadai nods with majesty and grace. "This is so. On etheric Tria Ra, babies are brought forth only when two Beings who are fully integrated within them Selves unite. Had you been an earth child, you would have had to master many, many lessons before you could have attained Being. But as you were born of two Who Are, you already are fully aware of All. All you need to learn is to freely express it."

My children, look down there: See all the presences, how they enjoy perfect harmony, yet are distinguishable from one another? That is Being. The union that exists is the result of the time when Light of the fifth dimension descended on all creation, ending all separation. It was an accelerated process that took place beyond the end of times. The ripening of planets took place and all previous experiments were declared complete. Genetic engineering ended its feasibility study and the result was the establishment of Heaven on Earth, or the Kingdom of God on the planet. But it wasn't always like this.

First was harmony, but no individuation. Then there was separation, but no harmony. The latter experiment is where most of our story takes place. There was suffering and abuse and misuse and mass amnesia. There was longing, hopes and prayers; each age was replaced with a new one. Countries reorganized themselves, borders dissolved and were replaced in a desire to establish new frontiers, forgetting that the Community they were looking for was with their own Spirit and that the borders represented their limited perceptions, to be removed and expanded to infinity.

People forgot who they were and what their purpose was. And yet, beloved Eliyanand and Aeterna, when you see what you are about to see and hear what you are about to hear, be forgiving; for to forgive is to love, and to love is to serve, and to serve is to Be.

So forgive the Big Bang on earth and what took place before it. Because it was merely a dream within Universal Consciousness.

Part I

THE VIEW FROM OUTER SPACE

Chapter 1

Doomsday

Hissing and crackling, the radio spewed out a steady stream of strident, shrieking voices, each cutting off the one before to grab the spotlight of being *the* voice of the news, no matter how bad: "Today, Donald Pagan warned the Reds that he will brook no further disregard of his ultimatum..."

Pagan still had in the shadow of his soul the false vision of an evil empire. "In the Reds' headquarters, sounds of preparation rumble ominously through the corridors of...megatons of...the Oval Room in the Pale House denies that...intolerability of checkmate status...unless these demands are met..."

Sighing, I looked out my office window overlooking San Francisco Bay. Everything was in chaos — even the water looked uneasy, roiling angrily in the wind. All sounds broadcast fear and impatience: the radio with its doomsday message, the grey naval boats tooting angrily. And all sights were those of panic. I tried to calm myself by focusing on the poster on my wall — a photo of a giant redwood forest, majestic and almost sacred in its palpable quiet, its spaciousness — but immediately my eyes wandered downward to the desk right below, where a copy of *Time* stared up defiantly. On the cover, Pagan and Popov (side by side for the "peace" talks) glared at each other in full, undisguised hatred despite the polite smiles on their lips. Under their faces was the caption: "Are We Going to Make It?"

Truthfully, I didn't know. How had we gotten to this pass?

We had delved too far into machinery and not far enough into ourselves. We used computers to communicate, forgetting what communication was all about. We substituted information *about* for the thing itself—we suppressed, rather than expressed, our fear, anger and other such emotions. We pulled apart flowers to analyze their function; we encouraged invalidism, and then dissected the corpses.

We turned ourselves into machines. Now we were at their mercy.

We had invaded, penetrated, violated the atom. We had awakened a sleeping giant, but we were not equipped to handle it.

"...Pagan warns that he will not be threatened...Popov is calling out his full armamentarium of..."

Something was wrong, very wrong. There was something out of balance in us. I could not say what it was; I only knew—by a feeling, a sensing—that it was so. As a child, I had had a sense...what was it? Something about Light, about being in nature; about—did it have something to do with floating? Or talking without words? Something elusive, ever receding before my attempts to grab it with my mind, my memory—but *something!* Some whole that was now shattered into fragments?

I was disturbed by the radio's bad tidings. I was in mortal terror. At the same time I heard an inner confidence within myself saying, "Be still and know I Am." What a paradoxical situation. Perhaps I was sliding into early senility or losing my mind. Perhaps I didn't know what I was rambling on about. Anything to avoid the inevitable—the end of everything.

But I loved the earth, and certainly all others must, too. Therefore annihilation could not happen. I still believed—I wanted to believe—that knowing more about the planet would make the difference, conquer the insanity. Thus I had studied and become a doctor, attempting to understand the connections between the mental/emotional structure and the physical structure. Thus I had researched the minutiae of the atomic structure, the macro-expanse of the planet's structure, and the human body that held both. Trying to find connections, trying to understand what causes disease, what brings about healing. Trying to heal.

But there was so much to heal. Disease was epidemic — AIDS, famine, cancers, depressions, congested cities. Human against himself, against his neighbors; power in the hands of overgrown children. False gods.

Yes, false identifications. A leaderless world, some said, where leaders became the exponents of moral revivals while their own tents were falling apart. It was the god of ownership that most of them worshipped. They saw all of earth as their playground by rights — to abuse, to gobble up, to destroy. Thus we all competed to deplete the earth: From the depths of the cohesive structure of the first concentric magnetic field (that is, solid earth) we extracted the nutrients (gold, silver, soil, iron) and put them aboveground. This made the earth less solid and the air heavier. So the elements, too, were out of alignment. As we ourselves were.

As I myself was. Like many others of my generation, I had spent my life in the pursuit of healing — but along the way I had gotten distracted from the original impulse to heal, to make whole. Relationships on the planet seemed stagnant. I recall a friend complaining, "I loved my wife with all my heart at first. But over the last few years it seemed we hardly talked about anything important anymore, only about where to eat and who to visit and what car would get the best mileage per gallon. We avoided each other's company — and yet when we had first met, what sparks between us, what longing to be one!"

It saddened me to think of our descent into the prosaic.

I wondered what my friends were doing right now. Were we connected by the networks, were any of them listening to the radio, too? Was this apparent final hour the time in which we were all trying to make sense of everything?

Was there something I had missed in my life, something I should have done? I thought back to my youth. I'd had misunderstandings with my sister, had yelled and teased; I'd had fights with my father when he told me what to do, and had railed against him; I'd been ignored by my mother, and in despair I had turned my back in contempt; I'd disputed violently with my teammates, had butted heads with my classmates, my teachers...

And for what? Was this what life was all about? Wasn't there something better, something more? I wished I had realized how much I had loved my sister, my mother, my father, my wife, my friends. I wished that all those hours first spent in arguments and later in therapeutic understandings would have been spent in joy and shared fun. I wished I had told them how much I loved them. If the planet went over the brink, there would be no more chances to tell them. I wished I had shown more love and been handicapped by less pride. I had had this one chance and I had blown it. We *all* had blown our one chance.

~ ❧ ~

"...Reds are said to be preparing for...Pagan, looking sober, will address the issue not with words but with..."

~ ❧ ~

What was my wife doing now? Did I have time to tell her I loved her? I picked up the phone. There was no dial tone — dead. At the same time, the radio began to splutter and squawk: "Mayday! Mayday!" Then silence. My heart contracted, my mouth was dry; I looked out across the bay and felt a sickeningly, deathly quiet. Then, realizing that my wife was gone from me, my parents gone from me, my friends, lovers, homes, landscapes, all chances gone from me, the end of the body, the end of the life, the end of the planet, the end of the world, I contracted into a ball of fear, I expanded into a fire of anger. I held the pictures inside me and outside me, cupped inside my memory. I let it all go, I imploded, I exploded

and the flare was blinding
"Here I go," I thought, not breathing.
I had seen light like that

but brighter
before,
and I thought, "Where?"
And then there was nothing...

Chapter 2

Outer Space

...but me.

I was still here!

Never had I expected this! When I'd seen the huge earth shatter into nothing more than boulders, and the boulders break into nothing more than dust—when that Great Final Holocaust, so long dreaded and anticipated, had at last occurred—I was sure with my last bodily gasp that that was the end of everything.

And yet I was still here.

My physical body was not here. My usual thoughts were not here. My usual emotions were not here. Yet *I* was here. What *was* this?

And *where* was this? There was no location—no cities, no mountains, no desert—nothing recognizable. Nothing to distinguish "here" from "not-here." I could not even say I was in "outer space"—there was no "outer" because there was no "inner." There was no boundary.

That which we knew as third and fourth dimensions, duality at large, had totally vanished as I found myself in a unified Light field nonrelatable to my earlier notions of space.

This was not outer space—it was spacelessness. And timelessness.

Slowly the veil began to lift, the memories began to come back, and I began to see what had happened on earth with complete and piercing clarity.

Had it really been necessary to blow ourselves up just to find out that we were immortal?

My awareness was no longer constrained by the bounds of earth; my Soul was free of its dense, barricading clothing (its physical, astral, feeling, and mental bodies). Thus I was free to take a clear, wide-angled look at the experiment, the classroom, that until recently had been known as earth (and was now known as the feasibility study on the Great Final Holocaust — the GFH).

So what went wrong?

We had fallen out of alignment with the Soul as humans and, forgetting that our true identity was Spirit, we stopped following its guidance. From there everything we had touched had taken a turn for the worse, away from the knowledge of the Soul. Traveling so far from our own Being, we had attempted to conquer, rather than respect, the Mysteries. We had set our sights on the immense and on the infinitesimal: Rocketing around the galaxy, we had come equipped with probes and flags with which to claim the unknowable as our own; homing in to the atom, we had pried out the secrets we did not know how to use. We had tried to rape God, to explode the At-One, blowing up the atonement to possess through reduction, through analysis, through violence.

We persisted for millennia with a patriarchal, dominating perspective that erased our possibilities of harmony. Both men and women were dominated by a perspective that made us all half-beings. Sometimes females rebelled with attitudes similar to their apparent other halves, and sometimes men gave up their characteristics to balance out the whole imbalanced planet. God remained impervious, of course. But we did violence to our Selves. The body — the instrument through which the Soul moves and acts — was no longer tuned to receive the Soul's guidance. Thus disconnected from its Source, the body ricocheted in abandoned terror, creating diseases that left no room for the bodies to live in. (At the same time the social body created social diseases called cities, which left no space for people to live in.) The exercise of awareness, cultivated by yogis for thousands of years — the breathing in of Soul Awareness as a basic means of communion — was replaced by computer communication networks.

Thus un-*inspired* (not breathed into), we let machines do it all for us. Instead of communicating directly, we placed our messages onto disks. Instead of dancing together, we exchanged disks on the subject of dancing. Instead of emphatic communication — singing, shouting, screaming in anger and in ecstasy — we diluted our emotions with technology. Telephone, faxes, radio, TV — these delivered messages faster than real feelings could. So we learned to respond to the false, and suppressed our anger, our fear, our sadness. We expected of life that it be a situation comedy; when it was not, we suppressed our rage and grief and contorted our lives to fit the script.

Most scripts were not precisely oriented to cosmic survival and multidimensional evolution. Most were small stories in which the majesty of the Soul had to give its place to the smallness of a third-dimensional narration that took itself to be the Whole. We thought that because we had a high level of technology we were more evolved than our forebears. We thought we could put everything we needed to know on a disk. And since data banks were so readily available, we thought we did not need to remember our purpose. Our destiny.

Forgetfulness thus blanketed the planet. It was an epidemic so widespread, so thorough, that almost everyone forgot that they had forgotten.

This was AIDS on the physical, a syndrome in which autoimmune signals were interposed in the DNA via a viral system that enabled people to destroy their bodies in an accelerated manner, not recognizing even themselves as Selves, since there was an imminent command for autoimmune destruction.

But there was also another AIDS. This was the Auto-Installed Divine Suppression by means of which people stopped seeing themselves as spiritual Beings, forgot all about the divine and divided themselves into exponents of diverse cults, viewpoints and sects, suppressing each other in the name of God.

Seeing this, the qualities of Essence living on the planet had gathered to help man recollect his true Being. From time to time, these qualities (mistakenly called "virtues") had put together an incarnate body. These messengers had, over a fragment of awareness, posed the basic questions to their fellow bodies. A few people took those questions to heart and were able to realize the truth about their Selves.

The embodied spirit took on the name of a Master and for some time left messages as a blueprint for Ascension to a higher perspective for living on this plane. Mostly, though, humans categorized the messages; they liked or disliked them, they found them interesting or nonsensical, they recorded them or threw them out.

Anything but take them seriously.

Part of the problem was that we did not know how to listen. The faculty of listening had been replaced by the faculty of translation: When we heard anything that differed from what we already knew, we either translated it to make it conform perfectly with what we already thought, or we denied that it might possibly be true. Thus, by crystallizing all of existence into one particular thought form and using that as a frame through which to interpret everything, we lost the ability to step outside of our circumscribed vision and hearing, distorting Reality and therefore missing the appropriate use of the seven levels of understanding.

And without this understanding, what a limited vision we humans had about ourselves!

First, because the clothing of the flesh eventually wore out, we saw ourselves as mortals. True, over the course of human history some groups on the planet believed in the concept of immortality—that there was Spirit as well as matter. But they saw Spirit from the vantage point of the laws of matter, which led to some rather gruesome circumstances. Some burned and tore the flesh—in order, they said, to separate matter from Spirit. These misguided groups claimed appropriately that the Spirit was eternal—that is, through all times—and omitted the guidance of their eternal Cause. But (as I see now) even time is an illusion.

Second, because we forgot that it is the Soul, not the pursuit of matter, that keeps us truly alive, we scrabbled and scrambled for money, for jobs, for position, for food. Those who stayed at that level have no bodies left to feed now. Out of touch with their Souls, they misused their bodies, vibrating them at such a frequency for the plane they were in that the elements broke their electrovalent and covalent bonds, and the crystals returned to their independent form. Instead of using emotions as a way of discovering their Soul, people used them as a drug — alternating between a fascination with the minor depolarization of microvolts in their nervous systems (excitements) and a depletion of their electric current (depressions).

And yet the whole purpose of feeling is to enter the Holy of Holies in oneself and to see the whole of one's nature!

On earth, fragmentation was all. During the time of what was called the Cold War, East had its piece and the West had its piece. In public they sparred like restrained roosters; but in private, they met to design how to enrich their mutual greed. Thus surface land was claimed; and from the depths of the earth, gold, silver, oil, iron and other so-called nutrients were extracted. This put air where solidity should have been, and solidity in the air — the earth's astral layer was filled with particles that belonged in the ground. Thus pollution arose, and the more extractions there were, the lighter the earth and the heavier the air became, and the whole equilibrium of the planetary and solar system was unbalanced. As the astral air was filled with carbon dioxide, carbon monoxide and other pollutants, its frequency became more solid, thus conducting all the communication waves floating around — radio, TV, satellite, ELF (extra-low frequencies that altered the electromagnetic force field of humans and animals, making them more susceptible to minor electrical stimulations) and so on.

In order to prevent the danger of miscommunication, the divine attributes of Essence took on bodily forms, presenting their one message in many ways. But this message, filtered through the heavy astral layer, was distorted: People used the information to promote their own cults and to attempt to destroy all other cults. What was thought of as communion was actually massive distortion. This distortion, due to the nearly solid astral air, also interfered with the cosmic rays entering the earth's atmosphere. The purpose of the rays was twofold: to awaken humanity to its connection with outer space and to rebalance the plundered earth. But the air had been too thick, the distortions too thick, the not-listening, the greed, the avarice too thick, the distortions, omissions and blunt generalizations much too thick. The messages had not made contact.

Not on the earth level.

The earth level — as I look from this plane at the great rocks tumbling through the universe with some discarnate survivors of the GFH, I can see that a new earth is already conceived — not only one, but many myriad possibilities of happenings. Alternate creation is constant, always pregnant with the next self-possibility...

Multisimultaneously, earth civilizations — Greek, Egyptian, Chinese, Roman etc. — are being created, generated, operated, directed or destroyed. Not the narrow view we thought of, but God (Generation/Operation and Direction/Destruction) simultaneously occurring. On earth we were used to viewing everything in terms of its form, but the heaviness of form has no place here. We need no longer make all in our own image. For there *is* no image now. All that is left is what *Is*, what was always obviously our Selves — the essential quality needed to reconstruct all form once again, or to not create a form at all.

Life and death — the notions of suppression — carry no weight out here. Free of the body mass, dressed only in my etheric robe, in a Light body, I now know that there *is* no destruction. The earth blew up, but yet here I Am. Forms change, appear, disappear; Essence remains, inviolable.

Did we really have to blow up the planet to recover our Selves?

Chapter 3

The Cat

"So now you understand."

What was this voice? It resonated throughout my being, sending ripples of awareness, of blissful, utter calm. Listening, I felt whole.

"Because I Am Wholeness. I Am All."

"And I?" I asked, having a sense of the answer even before the voice gave it.

"You Are the All as well. There is no difference. There is no duality and no separation."

"But..."

"Don't get caught up in the appearance of fragmentation. There is only One, in its various manifestations. You have already seen how humans brought about their own destruction on earth by forgetting their Source. So remember!"

I reflected on the greed, pride, anger, lust, envy, lies, fears, indolence, avarice, resentment, violation and isolation that characterized the human condition. I reflected on how even I, trying to be spiritual when I was on earth, had retained only a glimmer of remembrance — how I had lurched, fought and bludgeoned my way through life instead of entering the holy place of Source. And I said, *"I will remember."*

The voice permeated my Being. I experienced it everywhere. *"You have seen what you have seen,"* it said, *"because I told it to you. Now that you have this awareness, it is time for you to embody it in your own Being."*

"And how will I do that?" I asked in awe.

"You will be assisted by the attributes of Essence. They will enable you to express this awareness."

"But how will I know them?" I asked.

"You will know them," the voice insisted. *"They are qualities of your own Soul."*

"But if they are me, how come I don't already know..."

"You have forgotten the totality of the Soul," the voice said in answer. *"The attributes of Essence will help you remember Who You Are. Once you remember, you can integrate these qualities within your Self. That is what you long for; that is the task."*

Then all was silent. But still I could feel the all-encompassing presence of the Voice of Silence.

I had always felt a deep, sacred respect for cats, as had many others in many civilizations throughout human history. So I should not have been too surprised when the Cat showed up.

But I *was* surprised.

"The problem with your human race," said the Cat, not bothering to introduce itself, *"was that it failed to understand what the physical instrument was."*

I was caught off-guard. "How did you know I was interested in the physical instrument?" I demanded. I had been a medical doctor and a healer, a shaman or a priest over many lifetimes and through many cultures, having always been intrigued by the mysteries of health, healing and disease.

The Cat went on uninterruptedly, as if the answer were obvious.

"Not only did humans have a limited knowledge of themselves as Being, but they also had a limited knowledge of the machinery itself. They did not understand what the genetic entity of the body is."

Reflecting on my most recent life as a doctor, I recalled how my colleagues had considered illness to be a purely material phenomenon, a stimulus-response, problem-solving operation that denied the presence of the Soul; they considered healing to be the ingestion of chemical substances or the removal of diseased body parts. Nowhere did most of them — or their patients

—consider the possibility that diseases might have a nonphysical origin.

"Quite so," vibrated the Cat without speaking. So I realized that the Cat received my thoughts through the subtle frequency of my reflection on the subject; that I could speak or not speak—everything was always communicated.

Telepathy! In the instant that I experienced instantaneous communication, I was able to comprehend a mystery to which I had devoted many lifetimes: The real cause of disease was our fragmented view of life, which caused us to focus our attention on sheer survival and thus restrict our aliveness. This caused a deep uneasiness—a dis-ease—and our bodies embodied our restricted views by manifesting disease.

Dying, the Cat told me wordlessly, did not mean being extinguished, as humans believed and feared; it meant dying to a restricted density of understanding and being born to a larger dimension of understanding. Thus life was not a chronological, sequential, limited story, but a cosmic happening. A multicurring event. Here I was in outer space without a physical instrument, experiencing events with the Cat; and at the same time I was experiencing other events from my past—events tainted with what we humans call "honor" and "dishonor"—which were still occurring.

"Yes," responded the Cat. *"This has always been your inquiry: What happens in between events? Yet your education so far has been based entirely on explanations—not on the blank spaces in between."*

"The contexts," I responded.

"Yes, for lack of a better word—the blank spaces wherein the physical instrument displaces itself and can really be tuned."

I did not want to talk about the physical instrument. Now that I was finally free of the weight of the body and the physical plane, I had no wish to invite such confinement again. It seemed as if eons had gone by since I'd had a body! And suddenly I thought of earth, which no longer existed as I remembered it—and I recalled the beauty of the forests, where green had all the tonalities of green; where the ocean waves rushed in by the full moon's light; where my toes dug into the warm sand and the warm breeze caressed my face, and I was filled with the endless promise and passion of youth as my male body penetrated the voluptuous body of — what was she called? — Agna, an angel in delicacy, an animal in sensuality, reporting to my senses (in this wonderful physical instrument) what I believed was the most rapturous pleasure a being could ever have.

"Yes indeed," observed the Cat, *"you are still attached to a pathway to orgasm through the activation of a kundalini which is no longer here."*

I could not deny it.

"And more than that," it went on, *"why do you think the planet was destroyed? Because you all forgot the balance of the Whole — what you call 'health' — and therefore you ignored the tuning of the physical instrument."*

And so saying, the Cat disappeared.

Immediately it returned — in a form so huge that all of me fit on the tip of one hair of its tail.

I experienced a deep sound inside me; and as I vibrated, I was filled with a new awe and respect for this Cat, who could change size so rapidly.

Instantly the huge form disappeared and the Cat returned to its previous size.

"Yes," it said, rebounding up the vibration. *"That belief is what made your 'medicine' a failure. There is no such a thing as normal size. You humans reduced your own ideas of form to 'normal' and 'abnormal,' and the result was oppressive living, which caused so much anxiety to the whole of the human race.*

"Now that you have seen me so large, can you respect me and listen to me?"

I had no doubt that I was here with the Cat to learn a special lesson. I remembered what the voice had told me, and I wondered if the Cat was one of the attributes of Essence that would teach me about integration. I could have felt superior, special, being singled out for this teaching. But I knew that each Soul was somewhere/nowhere, interacting with somebody/nobody in its own useful way.

"Now watch," said the Cat, displaying a crystal prism. *"We will start to work."*

And I fell soundly asleep...

Chapter 4

Tuning the Physical Instrument

The physical instrument worked differently in ancient priitive cultures, which synchronized all their activities with the lunar month. This had an emotional effect on the body. But when civilization "progressed" to the point where people stored vital information in computer disks instead, the body's natural abilities atrophied. People grew careless and prideful: "Now that we have the disks," they thought, "we don't have to *live* our information." Thus they grew falsely self-confident about their own capacities.

So knowledge decayed into mere information. This information — kept in archives, out of reach — was rarely used, and thus the whole human race became disconnected from its natural power. The so-called primitive civilizations, using nothing more sophisticated than simple observation, had tuned themselves to the natural processes by regulating certain bodily functions according to their natural rhythms. How different from the earth when it blew...

"So," said the Cat, shaking me out of my reflections, *"are you willing to stop daydreaming your life away and start learning?"*

"I am," I said humbly.

"Then let us begin."

~ ❧ ~

"It has to do with Love," the Cat began.

Love was an element that nourished the Soul of all Beings. But over the course of earth time, those in authority forbade its open expression, especially outside the permissible contexts established by the Great Moral Order of the Ages.

These contexts were: (1) the mothering aspect (a vestige from primitive times); (2) the copulative aspect (necessary for procreation and recreation); and (3) the pleasure aspect (love for those actions directed toward the attainment of pleasurable goals).

There were a select few who discovered the forbidden art of Selfing, the art of knowing, loving, and serving the Self. These people disguised Selfing as spirituality, religion, psychic phenomena and transformational learnings, since the self-appointed leaders of the Great Moral Order sometimes permitted the open practice of such forms. However, because the leaders used only a material perspective for viewing reality, the few accomplished their goals only in a fragmented way. So feelings were separated from thoughts and thoughts from actions. Only true Love enabled the act of Selfing—engaging in the action of the Self. (I thought here of Agna/Bhakti-Shadai, my true love. She was the Soul with whom I had experienced the closest affinity throughout my lives.)

"Soulmate power," added the Cat, *"is still a minor form of the Light that is the reclamation power of Life itself."*

Most recently we had had that meeting and mating on the beach—then a long, long separation. She had evolved to the point where she was freed of the body and its wrappings, having been for many lifetimes an adept of the diverse initiation systems of the red-skinned people. Thus before the GFH occurred, she was one of a few who were chosen for a research voyage in a space capsule, the Starplane. From there she witnessed the destruction of the earth; this shocked her into forgetting her knowledge of Essence, of the continuity of Being. So she attracted layers of emotion to herself, and was crying for her loved ones from whom she had been separated.

(Little did she know that I, her lover, who kept her memory in the depths of the Soul, was a conscious survivor of this transgalactic event. How and where would we ever meet again?)

So the self-appointed teachers of transcendence measured the results of their spiritual work according to material parameters. Nevertheless, when the loyal forces of darkness were arguing nonchalantly about destroying bodies on earth, the teachings of these transcendence-mongers were as cries in the wilderness. Human values were low, and the act of Selfing held low priority in the days before our earth consumed itself in fire.

"So," I told the Cat, having received this portion of its teaching, "now tell me: What was inadequate about our tuning of the physical instrument?"

"Just because you are anxious to know," the Cat responded, *"doesn't bring you closer to the knowledge. In fact, your eagerness has been a barrier, blocking you from mastery of not only the physical, but also of the science of peace."*

"Peace?" I asked in surprise. "You mean what planetary governments used to talk about and lie about?"

"No, that was 'piece' — pieces to grab a hold of (as they did in claiming portions of the earth); pieces to rely on, rather than relying on Spirit. They were after true peace, but they misled themselves by thinking that what was needed was pieces of earth. Thus they forgot the integrity of the planet, since their own integrity had long since gone astray."

"Then what is the source of peace?" I asked.

"Patience, patience," advised the Cat. *"Your etheric body still has magnetic imprints of your erroneous habits from your earth life, even though you are now in 'heaven,' as you would call it. So we will have to show you the art of living step by step."*

I sighed appreciatively. How many times I had lacked the essence of peace! How I had longed for it!

"I am not the one who will teach it to you," the Cat said. *"This science cannot be learned from someone else — there is no one else. You already know there is nobody else,"* it added. And disappeared, saying, *"It all comes from within your Soul."*

I was panicked: "Cat, Cat, come back!" I cried. "Where are you? You were going to teach me something!" Oh, why hadn't I just listened, not taken the Cat for granted? Had I lost its friendship? Was I all alone in outer space? Had everyone perished or disappeared? Did I dream the Cat after all? Was I going out of my mind?

But I no longer had a mind. The mental body, the physical body, the feeling body, the imagination — all had disappeared long ago. Yet I couldn't even say "long ago," because there was no time here. There was no here here.

"Only *I* am here," I whispered to myself. And a ripple of energy moved out of Essence and vibrated through my etheric robe (the fiber that unifies the universe), which radiated and pulsed into all spaces, all directions. The ripple went beyond infinity. I observed myself as a creator.

"But what about the Cat?" I asked.

Instantly it appeared again.

"Oh joy!" I cried exuberantly, glad for the Cat's return. Then, skeptical, I asked: "What trick was that you were playing on me?" I answered my own question, recalling the dualistic methods of teaching on earth (stimulus-response, reward-and-punishment): "I know, you are *teaching* me something when you disappear, just like when you changed your size."

"Bah!" replied the Cat. *"Phenomena, phenomena! You always fall for them. You think it is 'the real thing,' like a soft drink on planet earth. Anyway, where are soft drinks now?"*

I would have been confused had I had a mind. Yet I accepted all these paradoxes — in a world of nonsense they made no sense; here they made sense. In my interaction with the Cat, each interaction built on the one before and was so whole that it rippled through my etheric field into infinity. I no longer felt any anxiety. Indeed, I felt a subtle sensation — hard to pinpoint — like allowing/enjoying — what might it be called...?

"Peace," responded the Cat. *"And that is what was missing in the tuning of the physical instrument."*

The step that was missed throughout previous earth evolution is now the next step for the whole universe. Transmutation at the cellular level is needed to allow the passing of Light into the system and to tune the physical instrument to a higher design.

"Do you still remember cars?" it asked suddenly.

Surprised at this apparent change of subject, I nevertheless answered, "Of course."

"Did you ever drive an angry car or an impatient, idle car?"

"Yes," I said, "and I didn't get where I wanted to go with ease."

"With dis-ease, then?"

I had never seen it this way.

"If you had a diseased car, you finally replaced it, eh? Even if you liked the color, the model or the mileage. Perhaps a friend told you, 'Don't you dare drive that car—it's a threat to you, your passengers, and other cars'—especially," the Cat added, *"if you never learned how to drive. Sooner or later, you took the diseased car out of circulation. Now, would talking to the car have made it change?"*

"No, of course not," I said.

"Well, that is not exactly so! You could have spoken in such a way that action could have been taken—maybe you could have repaired the oil pump, or even gotten a new one. Sometimes speaking in a wholesome way furthers action; however, that wasn't so on earth. Words there lost their meaning because people like you had forgotten them Selves. But if the oil was dirty or the gas was poor, sooner or later the car would have broken down again. Is that not so?"

"Make your point," I rushed the Cat. "What has this to do with us?"

"There you go, idling away again. You're at a subtler level, a less emotional form—but still impatient. The perceptions of your reality are the memory of a audio-video representation of life. See how short-tempered you still are? See how much cannot be learned when you're moody? Can't you see that as I talk to you I don't expect to go somewhere? In this void in which time does not exist, you call forth the nonexistent and lie about yourself, reducing life to form. Remember that this is nowhere, now."

And the Cat disappeared at will.

But this time I knew I could call it back at will. So instead I looked around.

~ ❧ ~

All notion of myself as what I had thought myself to be was gone. Stretching myself, I occupied all space, and instantaneously I saw from many dimension points. From one point of view I could see life on earth going on as it had before the bomb, as if all had been just a dream. From another point of view I could see the nuclear bang occurring. From still another point of view, slightly earlier in history, I could see the first pioneers who had come to earth as visitors. Thinking how nice it was to be in a new plane and wanting to secure their life on earth, they locked themselves into a crystallized form later called humanity. This crystal kept everyone imprisoned for eons; they dreamed of the stars from whence they came and built stories, myths, religions and sciences to blow themselves out into the openness of space once again. And all of this was *still* occurring while I was stretching into the immensity of my Self.

The vastness of the kingdom of possibility was becoming a true sense of life for this Self presence. I saw Agna aboard her ship — she could not see me, yet she remembered our encounter, which had so positively marked our lives on earth (since all encounters basically alter the foreverness of our encounter with our Selves). In this vastness of the open universe I also saw the myriad possibilities of actions that were offered not only to me but also to all who saw them. I freed myself to be Whatever I Am: the All and Everything of the reexpanded reduction of this massive point of view throughout the All of the cosmos, which I also Am.

Focusing myself down so that I could interact, I asked the Cat, "Please return."

It appeared, laughing wholeheartedly. I caught on to the magnificence of the revelation of this joke and joined in the laughter. "Seriously now, what is it you were going to tell me about healing and the art of medicine? What was it that we understood as such and called it 'gone wrong' on earth?"

And yet even in posing the question, as if the Cat were separate from me and possessed the answer that I lacked, I realized that I was All and Everything — including the presence of the Cat — and that in the aloneness of the Spirit, I needed the Cat to reflect back my Self.

So I posed the questions one after the other, and the

answers came from the space in which the emanation appeared through my etheric body.

The Cat added only, *"Questions and answers are like two sides of the same coin."*

So I remembered healing on earth. And sighed.

How to explain the utter ignorance in which humans lived on earth! They spent zillions of dollars on bodily adornment, but never fed their bodies correctly or even respected their Souls. Of course, the Souls ultimately were forgotten and the bodies decayed. Never was the Soul considered as that which empowers lives.

Lives were sacrificed for dollars, and no nation considered the fuel of loving as part of its budget. No money was spent on developing the feelings through which Souls could love their bodies, that the two might become integrated and life lived as a unity.

Fragmentation ruled the earth in nations, hearts, and minds. We had become so engrossed with matter that nothing mattered but materiality itself.

How had all this come to be? I decided to overview and track it back and find out. My purpose was a narration that, when telecast to a parallel earth that was still in existence, could trigger the people's Higher Selves to mobilize their Superconscious and by the power of Grace manifest the highest possibilities of Universal Consciousness so that it be fully manifested in all of our experience and thus shift the events in the earth I lived on.

How to find the humor of the whole and extinguish the fuel of the circumstances? I had to find a way.

"But," I asked the Cat, "if all is written and is true before it happened, why make the effort?"

"Wouldn't you prefer the story to unfold?" asked the Cat.

I looked within my Soul and saw the silence. In that deep Self there was a globe harmoniously designed for peace. So I said to the Cat, "Yes, my friend. It is time to rest and let our lives unfold."

Chapter 5

The Council of Twelve

Trillions of years ago I'd been in a similar situation.

Somewhere in the middle of Utopia (now here), in a place called Source (which, for all I know, still exists), the Council of Twelve Cosmic Individuals held a meeting to decree the end of universal peace. I was at that meeting.

For eons there had been a grand harmony, and all the universal networks benefited from it.

But there was a problem: The equality being experienced by all the elements was starting to erase all distinguishing features — it was getting hard to tell who was who. And because all the beings were the same, they did not need to feel, and so feelings were extinguished.

Mobility was the only thing that differentiated one element from another, and this victory had been achieved only at the expense of lengthy wars. Subsequent treaties of consolidation made twelve individuals the only real Beings responsible for all races and all forms of life. These *real* humans felt the needs for all the others, and experienced peace in their lives.

By "all forms of life," I mean the multiple life forms throughout creation. All have the use of diverse bodies for their displacement; yet they can leave their vehicles at will, merging into the Oneness. On earth this Oneness was called God or Essence or the Divine; but in truth it is the Nameless One — there is no one else to call It forth when It Is. It was this pulse of unity and easiness of life — which humans recalled as "paradise" and which all religions idealized as a steady state of no-conflict, no-growth and no-decay — that was controlled by the

Intergalactic Alliance, which in later time dimensions became a confederacy.

So at this meeting, the static state of the universe became evident to us all, and we realized that the period of consolidation had to end. Thus disharmony and fragmentation had been created to promote growth: The friction of the hearts would promote individuality; conflict would suppress the recollection of true identity.

From there I shrank into a "space vehicle" — a silver nonphysical body that enabled me to materialize through hyperspace and beyond. (Later on, on earth I found myself with an affinity for silver-colored cars.) I crossed stars and galaxies, taking the form of the territories through which I passed, like a cosmic chameleon. I reached points of concentration that ultimately landed me on earth's solar system (the "twelve-planet system," according to the Council). Before descending to earth, I destroyed populations from my silver battleship in order to create a magnetic block that would separate one world from the next. This block erased certain memories from the minds of the inhabitants of the twelve-planet system: the memory of life in Heaven and the memory that it was possible to rediscover this life. In its place I returned to each individual the responsibility for internalizing Essence, yet operating autonomously in life. Then at a certain point the vehicle disintegrated, and I became part of the population on earth; one incarnation in myriad embodiments was set forth at this time.

"Do not pretend to understand this adventure you have embarked on," said the Cat, interrupting my reminiscence. *"This adventure is whole. Simply listen to the enchantment of this process. Had your people been able to do that, they would have been gods on earth."*

"You mean there's still a chance for us all?" I asked eagerly, despite the fact that there was no longer an earth.

The Cat did not reply, but disappeared again. I felt I was losing the thread of my life. And yet, in separating from my earth life, I allowed for confusion — indeed, I welcomed it. For the first time I could truly accept the mystery of not knowing — of the unfoldment. If I *were* to know, the pattern would be revealed in its own way. I would find out not all at once but step by step, event after event.

For all I knew there was a sense of hope instilled in the true cosmic awakening process, even on my beloved planet earth. The joy of Ascension in Light and of the transmutation was a viable solution for the Mission on which I seemed to have been embarked forever.

The Cat reappeared.

Chapter 6

All and Everything

"The vehicle I have been talking to you about," the Cat began, *"the so-called physical human body, is a carrier that humans have spent lifetimes identified with. Because they believed that the body was who they were, they related to each other in a deluded, separated way rather than in the 'synergetic Oneness' of their Spirits. In fact, the qualities of Essence had gathered together a body specifically so they could travel through diverse densities as a reflection of the Self— as 'God's imagination.'*

"So when these essential qualities went forth into these diverse environments in which forces obliged them to appear in what has been called 'manifestation,' they built a mechanical system — much like a car, as I mentioned to you before." The Cat now appeared as a tiny kitten to explain in simple terms what it had talked about so complexly—that is, that certain elements of Essence consolidated in bodies in order to travel through the cosmos.

"Exactly!" said the Kitten. *"Thank you for teaching me your language."* And it recovered its previous size.

"See," said the Cat, *"because of the range of vibrations, you can interpret your own response to my communication. So I am talking to you about the construction of the vehicle; and your response to me — even though there are no bodies and no minds relating here — is to see a cat. But do you really know that I am that? Or is it only your association to the form?"*

I was confused—was the Cat only a projection of my imagination? "I'm sorry," I said.

"Never say you're sorry," the Cat responded. *"Just apologize. Who You Are should never invoke sorrow. Confess your ignorance*

on this matter, but don't call forth an identification with anything that does not uplift the wholeness of your Being. Understand: You Are! You never were! You always — all ways — Are. And any adjective you might use to describe yourself limits the multifacetedness of your Being. Be careful about the words you use; your language generates reality. Fortunately, from here it is easy to dissolve the slight frequencies on your etheric coat before they have any lasting, reshaping effect on your Soul.

"Do you remember when I disappeared for you the first time, and you were all alone?"

"You mean, all One?" I asked.

"Exactly — All-One. The All and awesome Oneness, or the One-in-All. I can take any shape, or none at all. And so with you. In this Light that you are, invoking any vibration allows you to take any form. This Light is Love — and some day you also will see it as Love, far, far away.

"This Light is what humanoids lived by, although they did not know it. There were some humans who had composed bodies that retained knowledge of their power of Essence. They tried to let the humanoids know about the Light, although they did not always succeed."

I remembered them — the Navigators. They had tried to teach people how to cross their self-imposed boundaries. "Tell me all about it!" I requested.

I was awed by the Cat's wealth of interlaced knowledge. My Soul was starting to experience a loving appreciation for this Being — a kind that I had never experienced before (at least not since the last meeting of the Council of Twelve). Yet it was not the kind of object-gratification love that I had known in my encounters with men and women throughout the many lives. It was more like being in the presence of the whole universe, but with an added bonus: with a singular "form" that interacted with me in a gentle but firm manner, and that allowed the mystery of this adventure to unfold. This enabled me to finally become aware of the Wholeness, not only because the Cat told me about it, but also because I had let go of the physical — the emotive-reactive thinking that earthlings were so used to, all that stuff tied up in a bundle called "my concern for my survival." So this kind of Love enabled me to listen and actually hear the Cat's explanations.

"Yes indeed," the Cat responded, as if he had heard my reflections out loud. *"When your words come from the center of your Being, there is no difference between reflecting them and saying them aloud. In both cases, there is the intention to direct them toward me.*

"Listen," the Cat went on, *"I also Am, just like you — and by Being, I hear Being. You can, too; the only reason you haven't done it so far is because you aren't aware of it. Do you know why? Don't answer, I know you don't. You don't need explanations throughout this universe — humans used explanations too much, mostly as excuses. Ultimately, most humans excused themselves from finally participating in their bodies with aliveness."* It continued, *"And so did you, as you well know!"*

"By becoming comfortable?"

"By becoming utterly comfortable! Remember before the Council introduced fragmentation? Remember harmony without friction, the beauty of the knowledge of immortality, the Love of the Soul, the peace of the environment? Sounds like paradise, right? But it was too comfortable! The Beings forgot the distinguishability — the distinction-ability — of their own individuation, and made no progress in the evolution of their Souls."

"Souls progress also?" I asked in surprise.

"Indeed. Refinement has no end. But we won't go into this until other events are cleared. The teaching must go at the rhythm the teaching wants to go at."

"You speak of the teaching," I said, "as if it were separate from us. But you showed me before that I was All-in-One, and therefore that nothing existed outside of our Selves."

"Curious paradoxes, eh? But remember the multisimultaneity of all things. You could grasp this truth better if you let go of the dimension of time. Time is a construction that, when seen from here, does not exist. So when we enter the domain of time, we can see all the eras, the epics, the events and so on."

"But we say we are 'here' — what is that?" I asked; then answered myself quickly: "Space. I can perceive you over there and me over here, and the pieces of rock where some surviving earthships are probably traveling."

"Toward where?" asked the Cat.

"I don't know—but still, the stars are all around us; and where are they if not in space?"

Instantly, all and everything became black. There was no Cat; there was no me; there were no rocks, no stars, no thing at all. The silence was total.

And so it remained.

I had lost the sense of Self; yet still I Was. All was still, all was static, all was without image. It was dark, and the darkness Was, and so Was I.

I heard a sound, a music coming from Soul, and in this sound I became absorbed. There was nothing to say about this sound—it was Spirit, or I had become it. The sound filled the darkness, and there was no distinction between the sound and the no-sound. So the sound was silence.

And so Was I.

The sound was silence, and the silence was darkness. But the darkness was All. So there was no no-darkness, and it all appeared as Light. And the Light was so strange and so all-pervasive that there was no no-Light.

Therefore I was Light.

Light was sound and silence, and I was all of it; and also was not, since there was nothing which I was not.

No distinctions.

There was no stillness apart from Spirit, but there was also no motion. Only What Was was. Only What Is is, and What Is Not is not, and also Is. Because only Isness is; but since no Isness is not, all that can be called Is had not been, so no more happening happened...

The event was ON
And silence Was again.

The peace filled the All and so pulsated that it all was
Being.
What causes Beings to Be?
The only cause — or purpose — is to Be.

And in this sound of silence, this Wholeness of Light, a Voice in the midst of the wilderness speaks the constant melody, the pulsating eternal harp, through all that will take forms: I Am — I Am — I Am.

And nothing else but that...

The silence of the Am-ness
eternal breath of life
continuous words of music
perennial sounds of love.

And the breath
imprints the self
ha ha ha

Ha I Am Ha I Am I Am
Haiam Haiam Haiam.

To Life To Life To Life

Chapter 7

Will

How long I bathed in the Wholeness of my Self I do not know. The pure joy of Being—its peaceful Wholeness, the tranquility of the voice of silence, and the all-encompassing expansiveness of the white Light—filled me, as I filled it, without distinctions. Then from within the Wholeness of the Oneness of the sound, I chose a point of vision and became it. Thus the Wholeness became vision; it was All, and it was me. Several times I made "my self"—the point of vision—expand until it disappeared, merging into the Whole. Soon I had learned how to rediscover, or create, my Self. And in the Wholeness, All That Was was also mine.

"Total inclusion," the Cat said.

The stars and suns reappeared; the pieces of rock carrying passengers traveling throughout the galaxy reappeared; and with it, all of space reappeared. "I am still timeless," I realized. "I wonder how this works."

"When you ask, you will be answered." And now the Cat's appearance as a cat was clear to me. And it was hilarious—to find, in the midst of the cosmos, an animal that I was familiar with on earth!

"Remember," asked the Cat, *"which was the most common animal in the heights of Macchu Pichu in Peru, around the pyramids of Egypt, in Teotihuacan, in the Roman forum?"*

"Indeed," I affirmed, "the cat." Cats had been sacred to earthlings from the beginning of time. So that was why this essential attribute who had been sent to show me my own Being appeared in what was, to me, a sacred mask. "Take off the mask!" I ordered, expecting a reply that would deepen the mystery even further.

"I did," replied the Cat, *"when you took off your own. Remember when there was no 'you,' no 'I' — when everything disappeared and merged into the All?"*

"Wow!" I exclaimed. It was true — when the Oneness manifested, there was no Cat and no I. "So there is no difference between you and me?" I asked, expecting the answer to be, "Of course."

But the Cat replied, *"No. I am a cat and you are a human. Essentially, however, there is only one Self."*

"But who lives in Essence? I thought that episode in Oneness would make the Self — my Self, your Self — only the *One* Self. But of course, that was an earth idea."

"It was so while it was happening. But now your Soul, which is covered by your etheric body, and my Soul, which is covered by my etheric body, allow us this dialogue."

"I want to know for sure: How can I have it all?"

"You already do," the Cat responded. *"Allowing it in your awareness is all a function of your divine Will."*

"Will? Where is it?" I asked, aligned with my Wholeness, which was feeding on the Love I had felt when merged with the Divine.

"Divine, exactly. Those two roads — di-vineness — are the roads to Being. They transcend space and time; they unite Love and Will. And now that you know this, you are ready to meet the other attributes of Essence."

Not human will. Divine One...

So this was what the voice had promised — that the attributes of Essence would appear to help me express the awareness of the One.

"But first," said the Cat, *"let me give you this gift."* And it handed me a piece of solid Light.

"What is it?" I wanted to know.

"I could say, 'it's you' — but for the purpose of this teaching, let us call it Will."

"Will, as in 'William'?"

"No, no — Will as in 'your Self.'"

Will's shape resembled what earthlings had called a double-prism pyramidal quartz crystal. Yes — "a crystal!" And as I called the word out, the crystal started to vibrate and the Light it had contained radiated out through space. "Thank you," I told the Cat. "But what does it do?"

As the crystal radiated a rainbow out of itself, the Cat responded, *"Whatever you want it to."*

I looked deeply at my Will — and again, as I had many times before, I saw the earth. But I also saw the stars and the skies, the survivors on the rocks, Agna sobbing, the silver spacecraft and all my lives on earth.

"The whole story is in here!" I exclaimed. "It's all everywhere, all happening simultaneously in a physical/metaphysical mosaic of sequential, aligned events of existing vibrations throughout the nothingness of it all."

"In this crystal," the Cat remarked, *"you can now hold what you used to think of as your Self — all the events with which you identified and burdened your Soul, forgetting Who you truly Are. The use of the crystal is the Will of the Soul, an attribute of Essence. You can have it — you can use it for travel and for learning — and yet you can still Be What you Are and be identified with nothing that is isolated from the Whole."*

"Oh, you mean I can travel into everywhere with this? I don't have to let it go?"

"It is your Will. But it isn't quite time to travel yet," the Cat said firmly. *"You still need to know more about navigation."*

"Navigation?" I echoed, recalling the many forms of transportation we had developed on earth: from horses to sailboats to steamboats to cars to airplanes to space shuttles — then came that GFH, and all had ended.

"Yes, yes," the Cat said patiently. *"You forgot only a few."*

"Which?" I asked in confusion. "Submarines? No, bicycles. No — yes — balloons. Oh, I don't know!"

"Once again, despite all your experience, you have forgotten the body," the Cat said quite seriously.

The body — of course! The Cat had tried to tell me about

the tuning of the physical instrument since our very first encounter. Once again I recalled all of what people had called technology, all of what old third-dimensional mass hallucinations had convinced us of, and with which we were totally identified: *Stuff.*

The real teachings had been given in the past by Masters who had consolidated qualities of Essence. But now Imago — the realm of falsifying imagination — had crystallized these once-living teachings in the form of structured systems. The heads of these systems were elected for a lifetime, and without understanding they preached the concepts that the Masters had actually experienced.

One elected king, who called himself the Navigator Pastor, placed himself between the world of the Reds and of Pagan. From his throne he preached the teachings of the Masters. His intentions were good — he *meant* to convey the teachings accurately. But like so many other humans, he had been corrupted by the mechanization of the world. So for the most part he forgot the purpose of his throne, and instead immersed himself in actions regulated by the laws of currency. Such actions were so removed from Source that whoever followed him had a chance of usurping his throne. This had happened for millennia, and thus all Spirit was reduced to nothing more than material wealth.

The Navigator Pastor knew little about navigating through the diverse realms of consciousness. Instead of voyaging within, he preached traveling throughout the world. He functioned as a buffer between Pagan's ambitions and the Reds' ambitions and was definitely helpful in ending the Cold War.

"Okay," I said at last, "I'm ready to know about the tuning of the physical instrument."

"Not yet, dear friend," replied the Cat. *"The voyage you are about to embark on is very long. You may remember a trillion years back, but you don't fully know what is stored in the memory of your Soul. Remember that you are Spirit and it has lived forever recording everything in the archives of your Soul. If the mental, physical or emotional bodies use this information to carry out their fundamental singular purpose and the real Life Purpose is forgotten,*

Essence won't manifest itself as such. This has happened so many times in so many civilizations that this time we are decoding your whole DNA so it will function. This time we need to make sure that enough of Essence is with you that you don't again forget your Self when navigating life's road."

"Enough of Essence *is* with me!" I declared. Actually, I thought I was *all* Essence.

"Of course you are," answered the Cat, *"and so is everything else. So were Pagan and the Reds and the Navigator Pastor. Remember the humans who ate each other's bodies — cannibals? They were Essence also. So was the nuclear bomb and those who threw it on each other's heads."*

"So," I said slowly, "Essence is not enough?"

"Yes, indeed it is. But look at Will — weren't you pleased to meet him, and at the same time to see Essence, your Self and also the power of the Light?"

I held the crystal in my right hand and looked at it. It smiled and entered my whole etheric robe. *"You will hear me if you see me as your Self,"* it said calmly.

And out of the crystal appeared a tan, robust, fair-skinned, tanned-faced Being, manifesting the powers that on earth were called masculinity. *"Will I Am,"* he spoke. *"I am your Self, embodying the power of Will. Will whatever you will, and it will Be. I am your quality of Essence known as the Will of Life."*

So I willed the presence of Agna. The vibration of my willing alerted William and aligned the power of Will to create a fiery thought form of her presence. *"So it is,"* Will responded, as she appeared. I looked at her — but she didn't seem to see me.

I turned to the Cat. "Why doesn't she say something?" I asked.

"Because she is not here. She is a holographic manifested function of the essential quality of your Will, as have been all rearrangements of realities on all levels of existence forever, including the one that is being experienced by you at this particular moment of code realignment," added the Cat to the reader listening to these words. *"By Will you can create and see, but for people to truly Be, they must be fully alive. As you can see by looking into*

the crystal, Agna, out there in that space vessel where you saw her last, nostalgically yearns for Life and is therefore grieving for her loved ones."

And William returned into the crystal. Yet I knew there was more to manifest.

"That is correct," said the Cat. *"You are doing very nicely. Remember, we are learning the science of peace, pax scientia; we want to make sure that when you are ready to navigate, you don't lose it again. In order to never lose it, it is important to stabilize each step. Other qualities of Essence will unfold in your life — and not in a material manner (as occurred on earth), but through the ethers.*

"See, the whole teaching is imprinted in the etheric fiber, and the fiber holds the Whole together. Therefore, by an act of Will, thoughts appear. That's how Agna, the fire element, appeared yet was not there: She was only in the mind."

This was different from when I looked straight into a point of vision, or into the crystal where all was stored. It was a...

"Thought," said the Cat. *"You have willed a thought machine."*

"A thought! But it looked like it had a form and a life of its own! This is not what we used to call thoughts."

"What you called thoughts were not true thoughts, only degraded images of matter. And yet some of you created thoughts that changed the world around! Remember Jesus? Moses? Buddha? Mohammed? Krishna? Ultimately, the Great Final Holocaust also originated in a thought which could have remained only an image had humanity awakened to its fifth-dimensional perspective and dissolved it into divine Light. But it manifested physically because on earth there was identification with the thought.

I was silent, reflecting.

"And now it will be good to be All-One again." The Cat instantly disappeared; and as it left, the stars were gone and everything went back to Spirit.

Chapter 8

More Earth History

People on earth had believed that anyone who spoke a lot about a subject knew more than others, and thus called this speaker an "authority." Over time, such authorities distorted the ability to invoke — they could not create by their word, only buy time in which to do their speaking. So whoever had the most money became the speakers, and thus the authorities. The only source of power at this time was currency.

Pagan, a world leader, seemed to be a good speaker; but in truth he was just a loudspeaker for an occult energy field which, from other dimensions, was mostly interested in distracting mass consciousness from waking up to true Reality. What really spoke through him were the concepts of survival, materialism, objects and Soul denial, which, surrendered to the prince of currency, had a life of their own. These concepts took precedence over human Beingness. But the leader was no different from the population over which he ruled — Paganism was the religion of the times, the ruling force.

Whenever people had a ruling class, they usually chose "the best" to rule — meaning those who were most developed according to the values of the times. And since there were no values that inspired, the worst were called "the best."

Some countries were filled with angry people who furiously resented anyone who was elected by the masses. (Little did they realize that "electing" occurred not only by voting but also by psychic emanations. The leadership matched and mirrored their subjects and these, not being aware, blamed the earlier ones for their own disconnected unhappiness. Thus they could maintain total irresponsibility for the quality of their government.) These people elected dictators who then reflected the fury the populace felt toward themselves by using torture, repression and punishment.

But for most of the planet's ruling classes, it was obsolete to consider sensations as valuable; monetarism was the most concrete form of feeling. "It is important to speak the truth," the ruler said in one of his speeches, "and the prophet that promises us redemption, progress and salvation is called money—profit is the Supreme Power and weapons are his angels. So we will take allocations for food, health, learning and shelter to pay our tributes to the Gods." Thus taxations were increased in order to sponsor their beliefs, leaving a whole group of homeless, elderly and sick without welfare in the so-called developed nations (this was not even a social issue in the so-called underdeveloped worlds).

Although people had divided opinions about Pagan, his actions proceeded to the end. More weapons here, fewer weapons there—the situation (seen from outside the gravitational field) made no sense. It was geared toward destruction. Suppressive thoughts about the survival of the bodies were implanted, and the result was a mistrustful population that lived immersed in fear.

Pagan triumphed, and a nuclear warhead was installed in each corner of the world for "protection." Against whom? I thought. (Later all warheads were dismantled and shared among the poorer nations of the world, from a concern about the number of unemployed warriors that could be left without work.) Humans considered this action either as terrible (because of the risk of annihilation) or as triumphant (because of the power over others it represented).

The few who saw it as a risk spent their lives behind bars—zoos for people—because they dared to speak as transmitters of any body of knowledge besides current reality (also known as absolute planetary truth). Occasionally they were visited by the networks, which broadcast their images throughout the world to exhibit them as exponents of insanity, treason or even humorous optimism.

"How dare they speak like that! Don't they know what the real world is?" asked Pagan's police. "They are evil, wanting to stop defense!" Thus the ancient custom of witch-hunting was reinstated, and toward the end the zoos were filled with dissidents. East and West each had their own zoos; and curiously enough, each imprisoned the opposite kind of people. Dissidents in the West were ordinary citizens in the East and vice versa.

The Navigator Pastor liked to say that we were all alike. He warned about the ill effects of nuclear action and prayed for peace. But he also lent currencies (with interest) to investors who built missiles, Scuds, Patriots, Exocets, Mirages, MIGS, B2s, H-bombs and other arms, which were hardly used for the furtherance of peace.

As the Pagan era was advancing in the West, the Red Patriarchs were advancing in the East. The Reds came from a lineage of rulers who had dominated the East for a long time. On the surface, this domination had begun only since the first Big War; but actually they had been the largest band on earth for hundreds of years. They had merely changed the symbols of one orthodox religion to another and, having long dominated the East, were now expanding into the West. The westerners were expanding into the east, the northerners into the south and vice versa. Only a few noticed that the extraplanetary ones were slowly but surely coming awake and deciphering their genetic codes. They were waking up to an identity that ("over the long run," as investment bankers used to say when coercing their clients into forgetting the present) would show itself to be the only eternal viable solution.

These Patriarchs were dying out, so to rejuvenate their rigid system, they decreed openness of trade. That may be why they finally collapsed, since Western influences were so unhealthy.

Their population began to worship the Lord of Money and fall prey to the highest cultural influences of the Pagan world — jeans, drugs and alcohol. The Paganites thought this heritage would perpetuate the memory of their civilization — they had nothing comparable to the Taj Mahal or the steam engine to offer. As the younger generations were absorbed by the values of the West, they threatened the rigid leaders, who then used all their inventiveness to collect missiles and materials and to advertise merchandise and food.

The last "peace" meeting between East and West had gone like this: Zaropov said, "What if we cut off all forms of communication so that our people are not contaminated by your thoughts?" Meanwhile he was preparing alternative networks of psychotronics with which to bombard the Western auric fields. (It had recently been discovered that beams of electromagnetic particles could enter the air space of another group and alter how people thought about or saw themselves and thus forget the structure of their divine Design. The earliest symptoms were termed "confusions of the mind," and later aberrant behavior became the norm. No promises given in those days had value, since they came from the lips, not the heart and thus had meaningful integrity.)

That was the meeting when the East and the West, realizing that there was a limited supply of matter, decided they had to get rid of each other. What neither side realized was that they could not exist without each other.

So at a summit peace conference Popov asked questions about how to live in peace, while intending to do only the opposite. Pagan accepted with a smile, which resulted in enormous impact for the lords of currency — the colas and jeans were bringing back what they called "hard tokens." These could be reinvested to enhance the P.P.

The P.P. ruled every producer's mind. Standing for Production Program, it actually meant Paranoid Projectiveness. The basic command was: "Destroy all competition! Militarize all zones! Prepare to attack as defense!" And the underlying value was: "If *I* don't survive, *they* better not, either!"

Power-Pushing was the rule of thumb — P.P.

Years before this meeting took place, an event had occurred in which the lords of currency had begun to take advantage of their power. The son of Ishmael (born to Abraham and Hagar, two characters who created a major split between the East and the West) decided to get black gold out of the skeletons of dinosaurs and raised the value of oil. The U.P.F. (United Paganistic Forces) applied the greed principle, which was based on the laws of temporality and gravitation, decreeing to all the people: "All that you must have and need, you can't have — but remember, you *must* have it!" This double bind drove humans to despair, and they obeyed — they gave anything to get what they "couldn't have."

Those were the days when the original death sentence — they called it "the energy crisis" — was programmed. From then on, everything went downhill. People forgot about trapping the sources of energy inside the Being itself, or at least inside the mind. They were obsessed with obtaining what they could not get, and therefore Paranoid Projectiveness grew.

So earth lived by three laws: gravity, temporality and currency. And the principles of exchange were a mere reflection of the karmic laws of the Whole. "Whole!" sneered Pagan. "The only wholeness is the wholeness of a coin! All the rest is gobbledygook." Karma — the notion of accountability — was ignored. It had been brought to the West by strangers, fit candidates for zoos.

The conflict *appeared* to be only between East and West — but simultaneously, a conglomerate called I.P.P. (International Power Pusher, a large network in the West) — was arranging to put anybody who wanted to be in "their" field of operation out of business. It destroyed governments of small states just as the Red Patriarchs did in the East via open military actions. There were basic similarities between the ways of the Red Patriarchs and those of the Paganistic Age.

Then there was the business of mind control. After the witch hunt, hundreds of smaller rulers of mini-empires ended up on a zoological-demonstration platform, exhibiting their acquisitions — the thousands of nonconformist dropouts from the West.

These mini-empires incorporated Churchianites, because they were under the laws of tax exemption. Perhaps their error was that they tried to teach to others what they themselves had yet to learn — to live in the world without being owned by it, yet still being ruled by the material laws. The Old Age was definitely collapsing, but the New Age spirit was, in actuality, playing by the same rules. All ended up isolated; only a few learned students got the real value of their teachers' thoughts. Yet even these students denied their learnings and their masters when their own survival was at stake.

In the final days they fought with each other in the zoo in the name of peace — swamis, rishis, yogis, sadhus, hasids, sufis, transformers, psychics and so on. They were well-intentioned people who saw a piece of the puzzle, and they believed sincerely in this piece. But they involved themselves unnecessarily in so many other things that they ended up prosecuted by the Pagans. Thus they became second-class dissidents in the West; the first class being reddish ("radish" — red outside, white inside) Westerners who inappropriately spoke the language of the East in the culture of the West.

On the other side of the world it was similar. Every once in awhile an Easterner would long for jeans and cola and the West's way of Paranoid Projection (which they called "freedom"). So he would escape from the East to the West, thus becoming a worldwide hero. He would be awarded, sheltered, protected and allowed to be a spokesman of the perils of non-monetarism in a so-called open way.

But in both the East and the West everyone watched over everyone else. So through gossip and intrigue, Paranoid Projectiveness was constantly enforced. Earth's condition was a sad one, and sad consequences came of it.

Throughout this time the Navigator Pastor traveled and sold subscriptions to his idea of God — the same God in whose name tribes, nations and individuals would kill, steal others' beliefs and burn and enslave bodies who refused to be enclosed or to live in a certain place just to serve the great religions of Churchianity. In this way he did violence to his own principles as well. Only a single growing force followed Spirit's direction and was fully committed to maximal growth — and this small group had its operating base in *each* and *every* life form of the universe. It was only a small starseed operation. Yet all seeds are *now* growing as we advance in this structural decoding of your Self.

Chapter 9

Precious Gifts from the Crystal

I listened to the crystal, which now constantly emanated a vibration toward the external layers of my etheric robe. This vibration sounded like "Will I am — William, William, William..."

"Do not get obsessed with the power of your Will," advised the Cat. *"William is an important but only a minor aspect of your Wholeness."*

I was utterly confused, as well as in awe. The Wholeness I had experienced — the essential merger of Self in All — had no attributes; and the merger of light and dark, sound and silence, were fulfilling as a Whole. But when William became present, I'd thought there was no room for someone else. The fullness was so great that I saw my Self as Whole.

"It seems you relate to jewels," said the Cat. *"You remind me of what the Greeks required in order to be Whole: Each quality was made a God, but only so they could listen. Therefore I will give you a bag of stones. They are very precious. Later on, in due time, you can pick them out of the bag, place them in your field, and* ***become*** *the quality of Essence that you like. When you have them all in you at once, you will become be-you-to-full."*

"Be-you-to-full — what is that?" I asked, never having heard "be-au-ti-ful" pronounced this way. Beautyfull."

"I'll show you," said the Cat. *"But first you must know that each quality is Light. Move the crystal, since this white Light of the crystal has all Lights, and you'll see."*

I turned the crystal in my hands and lo and behold, a blue-green ray of light came forth. There were other glows as well, but this ray separated itself and appeared as a sparkling aquamarine jewel. Out of it came a Being that looked female in form, but clearly was divine, not human.

"Who are you, precious one?" I asked.

"I am your Beauty," she said as she grew to an enormous size, large enough to fill the firmament. Her hair was blue-green and her halo was blue light. She looked like the presence of a great angelic fairy, surrounded by golden dust and enveloping us all.

"Can you appreciate me?" she asked. My arms had fallen open, to fly.

"Yes," I answered, and flew up to be closer to her face. "Yes, indeed."

"This Beauty," said the Cat, *"is actually your own beauty, just as William is your will. When you learn about all the qualities of Essence, you will no longer reach for her. You will Be-You-To-Full."*

Be-you-to-full — that was what it had always meant: Fullness! Those people on earth who were fulfilled were beautiful, and in their satisfaction they had enough to fill them up. They were distinct from the "pretty" ones. I always knew that there was more to esthetics than shape.

"Correct," said the Cat. *"The being-you-to-fullness will allow you to navigate without danger."*

"I am your Beauty," Beauty added, *"and I am here to stay for you to enjoy."* She remained within an aquamarine globe inside my etheric robe.

"You are showing and giving me so many precious things," I said gratefully.

"They are yours — and it is your gratitude that allows the magic of this world to continue. Without it, all goes stale. Which is what happened on earth: Again and again people took situations for granted, which thereby degenerated into lifeless memories. As with crystals, stones and gems, they vainly collected them, giving monetary values to what was real in value and calling prosperity the amount of collectible, third-dimensional objects to compare to others' quantities, redefining wealth as stuff.

"Grace is all that binds us. I am here by Grace alone. Your Grace is the use of your Will to thank your Self, through me, for

What you Are," the Cat ended. And it disappeared once again and left me alone.

But this time I had company in the completeness of my aloneness. Beauty and Will, in their precious essential forms, were floating in my field. As I looked into the crystal and the gold, I rippled a wave toward the region of my thoughts and a flower appeared — a Purple Rose.

"This is Spirit," said the Cat.

I smiled as the fragrance of the mystical universe represented itself via the Purple Rose's fresh dew expanding through my field. The smell rippled toward me as I opened my heart to it. And the more I opened to it, the more it grew — suddenly, the whole universe was a Purple Rose with aquamarine drops of beauty on its petals and distilled vapors that shaped all ripples of my soul — all motion in all things.

I heard my Soul sing:

"Ecstatic sense of Self,
beloved flower of life
among the stony planets,
remind us Who we Are.

Ecstatic smell of life
the power of creation
through Will now manifested
into that, That I Am.

The power of creation is a function of William and Beauty, I reflected.

"Well," said the Cat, instantly appearing, *"it seems I can't leave you all by yourself. You draw conclusions too easily and too fast. How about just* ***enjoying*** *what is present* ***now!"***

I took a deep breath. The flower disappeared, and all because I Am.

Chapter 10

More Gifts from the Crystal

"Now is the time for me to recover the lost art of navigation," I told the Cat.

The ancient ones had called it cybernetics, although during earth's last days this had degenerated into mere feedback mechanisms.

"And why," asked the Cat, *"do you think you are ready?"*

"Because I am starting to comprehend how unless we have a clear understanding of who we are as divine, transcendent Beings, the qualities of Essence — be they Will or Beauty or others — have only a psychological nature. That explains why on earth people lacked the fire of Life. The spark of Being was hidden (we were falsely impressed by such misused terms as beauty or will), misinterpreted by shapes of physical forms to which in the last days all became addicted to, whether in the form of obsessive body-shaping through starvation diets and heartless exercises or the willingness to control our minds and destinies with no higher purpose than the body-mind apparatus. We could not become Whole by adding all the parts. Wholeness means *health!* You asked me earlier why I thought earth's medical systems did not produce their intended results. Then I didn't know — but now the answer is simple: Health can only be in *Wholeness,* and Wholeness is a function of knowledge of one's Soul. If you don't have knowledge and follow the guidance of your Spirit, you can't really learn to drive the vehicle that is the living body, the physical instrument. You can only perform a mechanical action, in which the true homeostasis is never found."

"Undoubtedly," said the Cat, *"your understanding will assist*

you in seeing why, in the lifetimes when you were a healer of the body or mind, so many misleading actions were taken."

For years, the healing arts on earth believed that the body was the only thing that made a difference. Later on, some knowledge of mind was added, but this was misunderstood as the person's behavior.

In my most recent lifetime I had been a physician. My interest in searching for my Soul had taken me into medicine; I wanted to enliven the Self into its own process of healing. I knew there was a stage in being human that, when awakened, could breathe the fullness of itself and handle the distinctions of the various forms of Being. Yet in my searches on earth, everything appeared fragmented; East as well as West had explanations for "the fall of man" (which I thought of as the loss of the Wholeness into fragmentation). Such an explanation only filled the human race with nostalgia — there was no way of proving how it had been, so it was impossible to return to how it was. All seemed to be historic and based on the time line. No one seemed to discover in real life what physicists like Einstein, Oppenheimer and Bohr were describing in quantum physics. A divinely inspired physicist named Hawking wrote a history of time which came close to nonlinear, multidimensional global understanding, but people thought of it as a brilliant theory, no more than that.

Systems were studied to explain the composition and functions of the organs; some saw the body as all matter, others as the interplay with energy. Each looked at the others with disdain, and any search for the Essence was unsolved. Schools of religion and mystical awareness had their explanations, but often took them as tools for controlling their followers' mental bodies (who keenly rearranged their realities to fit the models rather than to discover their own elevation of truth). So the qualities of Essence were lost.

"So now, dear Cat, I see that what was missing made us blow up the earth. Humanoids treated one another as objects made of flesh that were activated by electrical currents, but never as Gods. Responsibility for their Beauty and their Will they ascribed to 'character determination,' never to the Self. And they showed these qualities proudly and protectively."

"This is correct – but aren't you judging prematurely, from only **some** *attributes?"* asked the Cat. *"Do you remember the bag I offered you? Have you reached inside to find out what it holds?"*

"The bag – of course! Where is it?" I wondered.

"Where all is kept – in the crystal."

I started rubbing the crystal; and as I polished it, Will invited me inside.

"How can I contract myself to your size?" I asked.

The crystal smiled and grew so big that all the galaxies fit into it.

"The dimensionalities of size," said the Cat, *"are such that, even though they seem to reveal a sort of hierarchy to you, what is great in one dimension can be nothing perceivable in the next. You were used to the three dimensions of your world. Here you saw the fourth, through time; the fifth, through space; the sixth, in Oneness; the seventh, in your composite, undivided divine Essence; and the eighth, in the aggregates of the Group Soul, where many zillions through creation act as an operating unit for the work that goes beyond the beyond. The seventh plane is the first launching base for synergy,"* added the Cat.

And right in front of me (in what is now called a holographic, omnidimensional, pluridirectedness, nonentropic alignment) every created object that existed, as well as those not yet thought of, "moved" in perfect alignment toward a goal known only to themselves while coexisting with all levels. It was the *non plus ultra* – simultaneous light-and-sound fireworks! It was more spectacular than I had ever dreamt of.

On a giant screen like a mandala or a cosmic Tibetan-like tanka from which boddhisattvas and buddhas emanated in all sizes, activating my memories of the encounters on late earth with the Dalai Lama, I could see in depth my Self and all Selves being born and growing and dying and being born again in all shapes and times and forms, in all worlds simultaneously – inside the crystal that was called my Will and the aquamarine ball that was called my Beauty – all interconnected, simultaneously existing and yet not influencing or intermingling with one another. Each element was respectful of the decision that each other element was making in its own time-warp. All was held perfectly in order, an order that I could not conceive or understand – the order of the illuminated vision of a perfect diamond. The reflection of each facet infinitely perpetuated the reproduction of this scene.

I returned to my own etheric field.

"Never," said the Cat, bursting with laughter, *"will you know from whence the new surprise appears."*

A perfect diamond appeared in my etheric robe, floating with the crystal and the aquamarine. It reflected the white Light of Clarity.

"Follow the reflection," said the Cat. I did, and it led me toward a blue light emanating from the center of my crown. There – inside my etheric "head" – I found the source of this bluish ray: a small blue pearl. Seeing an older man appear, I smiled.

"I am the essence of your Wise Self," he said, *"and am called Augustus. I hold the correction of all actions that have taken place. I have lived forever, and after erring and forgiving I learned the lessons and became Wisdom.*

"For years I spoke through prophets down on earth and on other worlds. Some who listened to my words mostly admired the length of my beard or tried to apply my teachings for awhile but later succumbed and made profits of my prophecies, becoming churches that surrendered to the law of currencies. Few really heard me. I humbly beg you to listen, because what I am about to say is older than time:

"I am the **deja vu** *of experience, the truthful advisor who knows best. Many times I work through the sharpness of the diamond, cutting through with intuition or vision or intellection. Those are the times I have to activate myself.*

"But truly, I filter the listener," he went on, *"and I sit above the angel of your crown – that which looks like the spheroidal structure of your bones when you spread your arms."* Then he opened his arms and caressed my inner ear, relaxing me with the wind of peace.

"The Wisdom I Am has always been; it belongs to all and has

remained with man. Yet his deafness caused him to become his own judge. Thus you no longer have a planet to play in."

"You seem so familiar to me, Augustus," I said, "and yet I know that you know more than I can ever comprehend."

"I am your Self, as I am the Essence That I Am. But my qualities could develop only when the obstacles that obscured me were cleared," he said, folding his arms and body and entering the structure of the pearl. *"You will learn what needs to be learned, and even more.*

"I know you feel grateful and rich; every human being, not only you, has all these qualities and more. So you may ask yourself, why did suffering occur?"

"The mystery, beloved Soul," interjected the Cat, *"is yet to be disclosed."*

I wondered: Did rulers, kings, priests or even millionaires ever conceive the possibility of their real wealth? People always tried to possess diamonds, gold, pearls, crystals. And here I was, having them in a place where matter doesn't exist! And where it doesn't matter, there it always IS.

Did I need to die to be born again? Jesus had said so, but people thought of death as a matter of the body. There was also the possibility of a *graceful death* — a crossing through the bridge, the tunnel between dimensions — in order to assert the majesty of the fifth-dimensional Self. Majesty?

Perhaps the ancient kings had known — they had crowned themselves with precious stones.

Some of these thoughts rippled through all the gifts I had received so far, appearing in a kingly crown: the crystal Will held, the aquamarine Beauty, and in the heights shone the diamond, holding the wise blue pearl in its depths.

"What is the bag made of, that it contains these precious gifts?" I asked the Cat.

"You could say 'contains,' but maybe for your purpose you could say instead, 'reveals' or 'unveils,'" it answered.

"Veils?"

"Yes, since you can perceive them only when you are Who You

Are; then they appear for you. It's like a council, do you understand?"

"So we all have it All, and we veil our Selves and our attributes by the ways we hold our Selves and tell ourselves to be...the idea we have of our Selves," I said.

"If you hold your Selves as bodies (which is how all survival dynamics on earth were conducted, since all they cared about was keeping their bodies going), all that is subtle is simply veiled. If the reaction of the bodies creates frictions in the environment, the bag is made of feelings; then all that's subtle and beyond feeling becomes veiled.

"You saw what thoughts can do—you brought Agna forth without her Life, and therefore her Essence was also veiled for you."

As the Cat finished talking, I replied, "That is true. Truth seen in each level presents a level of reality in itself. Held in the context of feeling, it all shows up as this or that..." As I spoke, an eight-pointed emerald spiraled out from my heart.

"This green jewel is Truth," said the Cat. *"It brings you harmony and opens the gates to Love."*

Androgyny sprang out of the emerald and spoke: *"I am all genders. I vitalize the seed of God, and only through me can Love flow.*

I vitalize the heart of man,
the sense of woman in each man,
I vitalize the sense of male
in each female I enthrone.

A green light spread out and awakened the presence of the Purple Rose. Androgyny sat in the light, and the emerald located itself in the center of my etheric heart. Gold appeared, like the earth metal, but warm—and it said:

"I am Love, which fuels the Truth,
kindles the Beauty,
Wills all the Power,
seeds the true Wisdom,
shining the Light.

And the Cat let the remaining gems out of the bag: There was the golden sapphire of Certainty; there was the blue sapphire of Compassion; there was the silver sword of Authenticity; and the stardust of Forgiveness. And that — along with the crystal Will, the aquamarine Beauty, the diamond of Clarity, the pearl of Wisdom, the emerald of Truth, the Purple Rose of Spirit, and the gold of Love — made eleven essential qualities.

"Here's the twelfth!" exclaimed the Cat, turning ruby red — a scarlet, winey, bloody red — and saying:

> *I am your Self,*
> *a gift of pure Strength,*
> *the animal nature.*
> *Purest grounding*
> *of power and movement*
> *brings forth the ruby that I Am*
> *for you.*

And a beautiful, grounded, rounded ruby appeared, reflected in the halo of my Soul, revealing at last the balance of this action.

Now I was alone with all these parts — yet they were not parts, but wholesome gifts of a divine nature. I sensed that I had lost a friend in order to own an expression of my Soul. Yet I knew that now I had a friend forever — not only one, but my own Council of Twelve!

Chapter 11

Embodiment Plans

Throughout the previous encounters with Spirit, I had begun to think; and in this thinking, a new dimension of Being had become possible. Augustus, who had been sitting in the blue pearl of Wisdom, broke his silence to stand in front of my etheric field. And even though all qualities of Essence empowered each thought, I realized that the ability to have Life was not complete without being in a body.

"You mean a physical body," said Augustus. *"Because from the moment you engaged with us, the etheric body started filling up and your thoughts became the mental field of Self-expression. Now you have even created a mind for yourself, first by the power of Will, and then with the assistance from all of us."*

Beauty interceded on my behalf: *"He means a* ***feeling*** *body – that through which he could connect to imagining (image-in-action) the physical."*

"'Physical' and 'feeling' don't exist when images aren't present," Androgyny said truthfully, in the most balanced and centered way. *"This divine androgynous quality was the element that the planet was about to receive toward its completion days. Mother Earth balanced with Father Spirit so that it became an androgynous planet, giving and receiving powerfully and sensitively in a paradoxically harmonious manner. Only in positive imagination can you select the grossness or serenity in which you want to reside."*

I, the silent witness in this show, was amazed: It seemed like my destiny would be controlled by the Will of the forces, not by my own will. But then I remembered that *I* had brought them forward by agreeing to be my Self, and that what this truly implied was the openness to continually Become instead of just statically Be.

This realization brought forward William, who said humbly, *"Please instruct me about what you want. All the qualities of Essence are here to serve you in the ever-expanding co-creation of evolution. The only one who has not yet realized this is you."*

I was used to receiving my instructions from the Cat, so I called out, "Cat!" —but it just stood there, smiling at all the possibilities, knowing (better than I) that it was up to me to choose where to lead this voyage. This is called the writing of the script through which, from one dimension to the next, the vehicles follow their previously aligned pathway.

The diamond made itself present, and its light illuminated the power to know. Thought was a powerful expression of my Self, and true creativity would manifest through this freedom of expression.

I was in the presence of my Soul's court; I lacked only a sense of identity with Self. Not that I wasn't present —I was simply missing a fragrance in which my choices (correct or not, reasonable or not) would bloom for all of our highest good. All was laid out as ripples in my field, but it was the Wholeness and fragrance that gave meaning to the Whole.

And thus the Mystic Purple Rose appeared and said, *"I am the vehicle of inner connection. I am eternal, the Spirit itself, the kindler and mover of messages within. Without my nectar, even the essential qualities of Self, and the Soul itself and all that exists become disjointed. My purple flaming Light transmutes the separateness and makes it Whole. The smell of the rose calls forth the love called Spiritual Love, in which we all can breathe at ease. Cohesiveness is what I bring you,"* it said, as all the qualities and attributes relaxed in its dewy fragrance of interconnecting Love.

The clearest thought appeared, and all the qualities aligned behind it. I was for the moment stunned by the enormity of what I had been given —the bag of jewels and the powers they contained. I queried, "Why have I been chosen? Is it because I am so special that I have been given these gifts?"

"That," said the Cat soberly, *"is the wrong question. That is the birth of the separate alter ego, the realm of Imago. Any question from the alter ego blocks the flow of energy and leads to false*

answers. Thus a self-perpetuating delusionary system of the reflective mind arises that prevents the true Mind from manifesting."

"The true Mind?" I asked, humbled.

"Yes, the true ***Ego*** *— I Am."*

So I set aside my notions of specialness: In the presence of the qualities of Soul, there was a work to be done. "Then let there be All," I said, "in the order the universe proclaims. I accept its function. I humbly accept my greatness. Let me be clothed with all the robes — etheric, feeling, mental, physical — and let me know what I am to do."

And I found myself dressing up with the garments of all worlds in what is called the Presence of the Lord.

I mounted a staircase of Light till I reached the presence of a gigantic throne. In front of the throne like an enormous candelabra there were the Elohim, Beings of Light confirming the nine arms of this candelabra. There on the throne of Light sat the Eternal Being of flaming golden Light — the Ancient of the Ancients, the Elder of All Times, surrounded by angels and archangels who chanted, "Holy, holy, holy, heavenly hosts sing your glory."

I humbly ascended and merged for an eternal instant with the Being sitting on the throne, and as this took place I knew forever that I myself, as all who are invited and accept, was, am and always will be a Christed entity, a Lightbearer for all worlds, an anointed being of Source.

The thoughts whirled around the mental body, knitting it together with power derived from all thoughts that had ever been uttered — not only by my Self but also by the Wholeness of Creation.

This was so intensely fascinating to experience that I knew I had become forever aligned consciously in the One and only probability of Source — just as fascinating as it had been to realize how I had connected with the Cat in the timeless etheric field when I became conscious of the planetary dream that we had engaged on earth to teach ourselves the lesson of Totality. The mind conceived of a before and an after — a very mechanical construction in which every thought creation located itself in a sequential association, fixating the idea into its surrounding field. It looked like a motion picture of events, bound by form and space.

The experiment was on! I called William to test whether I had control.

William laughed. *"The Mind appears, and you ask about control! Indeed, you created it by one thought, but now you are scared of your own creation.*

"No thought ever can affect the Wholeness of your Soul – but you must watch its evolution. Awareness of your creation implies full responsibility. Anything that enters the mental self evolves beyond Mind and turns to matter, if allowed. It is in the possibility of Mind, no matter how infinite this appears. This is almost an infinite realm, since it is only Creation," he said, showing me in the crystal the extension of Mind.

It was immense! It reached the wholeness of the mental plane, zillions of light years' worth of journeying; but it was held in the fragrance of the Purple Rose – the "spiritual container larger than the mind" – and therefore a master of it.

"This is very important," I insisted. "Because when I was on earth, many believed that the mind was God. We called God 'universal mind' and, admiring its virtues, we relinquished our control as people."

Islamic people used to shout that God is greater – Allah Hu Akbar – placing creation in the context of the Almighty.

"Such control," answered Augustus, *"was never considered as belonging to the Soul. Bodies and feelings, with their intermediate images, were thought of as the Self and were held by thought forms, which crystallized all of life in a rigid way and manifested behaviors that separated the human instruments from each other time and time again. People never learned that the crystallization in which they were held was the controlling form of* ***one thought*** *– the mass consciousness of humankind, from which there was no escape."*

"Many forms of mind control were taught," added Androgyny, *"but most had to do with the ownership of people. On earth slavery and suppression of bodies were a way of being."*

"And needless to add," added the Cat, *"those bodies were scarred like old cars after many wrecks. They were useful only for enriching the soil in graveyards."*

Souls had been trapped in these crystallized forms. Without knowing who they were, they had left their bodies through the phenomenon called death, but still imaged themselves to be on earth. Then they were either drawn into another incarnation because of some vice or obsession or they kept floating in the realm of imagination (a grosser robe further down the line of robes covering Essence), trying to control another body. Thus they might possess a body from a discarnate level, ruling over it without caring who it belonged to. These fourth-dimensional entities or demons, as they were called, were sometimes forms of feelings or thoughts that acted like interference signal, emanating a frequency that blocked the transmission of the Light.

Many a lonely person channeled them and served as a loudspeaker for incomplete cycles of living. Their consciousnesses streamed through the host Selves, thus causing aberrations.

On earth I'd read some literature on ghosts and zombies. I hadn't taken their existence seriously. I had, however, watched the faces of politicians and asked myself, "I wonder who runs them." I couldn't understand how they couldn't see that aligning their currencies behind instruments of destruction would destroy them also. They seemed not to care about bodies or lives. Infants, babies, women, men—people didn't seem to matter; only their own ideology mattered. Now I could see how in their own ignorance they were subject to the control of crystallized thought forms (such as the current ideology), which meant that when any thought that seemed to oppose their ways was presented, they would be angered.

The mental realm was organized under the dominion of a few basic three-dimensional thought forms which—*"from the perspective of the Soul,"* explained Androgyny—were meant to structure the plane. Examples of these included *gravity* (further grossness through the ethereal), *exchange* (the exchange of impulses that cause a giving and receiving) and *time* (sequentiality of operation). But people lived by these three regulating thought forms as if they were absolute laws, and anyone who tried to defy them was legally punished.

How could these rules have been so misinterpreted? The density of matter seemed to make time an enemy, in which beginnings and endings (that is, changes) were to be avoided; the exchanges, which were measured in money, made currency the lord of exchange; and because humans had forgotten about the Soul, these laws were larger than man. Thus the qualities of Essence could penetrate those thought forms only when they were truly lived and embodied.

"Thus the search for God, virtue, wholeness, transcendence or whatever became a search for Truth in a realm that knew only relative truth," said Augustus. *"Just as you — even once you knew your Self — had no power without the Purple Rose, so mankind had no chance to find itself without the Wholeness of the Spirit Self."*

I understood. No wonder the Cat said that I wasn't ready for the knowledge of the tuning of the physical instrument. No wonder all those schools of medicine taught in a way that prevented any real learning. No wonder that even when they spoke of holistic health, what they really meant was 1 + 1 = 2, instead of truly seeing the Whole. "To make the world work, what was needed was a distinct, all-inclusive way of Being — at least," I said aloud, "all-inclusive insofar as the pattern was revealed."

"And still that is not enough," said the Cat. *"You needed the Great Final Holocaust as well. It's almost as if the GFH was your only chance to listen and see — your behavior on earth was so forgetful and reactive that the influence of your upbringing and the psychological elements of love needed to be healed before you ever could see your feeling robe. People on earth used to sense feelings, but they rarely truly felt. It is through the power of the Soul that the feelings can come forth, and only in that way can enlivenment occur."*

"And of course," added the Rose, *"we will use your life memory as a pattern to clear it up. Then, once you have seen it clearly, we might prepare your life's surprise."* And GFH could instead stand for God Following Heart, or spiritual survival of the dream.

And the Purple Rose folded up and ascended — its violet

aroma radiating from it – into the arms of Beauty. A wonderful place to rest.

Chapter 12

The Seven Lower and the Five Upper Wheels

There was also a wonderful place to rest on earth, where universes expanded into each other like the embrace of two losing them Selves and admiring both the sameness and the uniqueness of the other.

Earth life had its romantic aspects, and most actions and interactions were ruled by an element called feeling. This element had sometimes been the cause of wars — and many times the cause of the desire to be alive. Helen of Troy, Marie Antoinette, Cleopatra and so many other women had precipitated intense conflicts over feelings.

I needed to discover how it all had come about.

I called together my council and asked for Wisdom. Augustus made himself present.

"If and when you enter the knowledge of the feeling realm," he said, *"great winds will be stirred up and the peace you now enjoy will be challenged."*

But the team supported my inquiry (which was a mixture of interest and curiosity), so Augustus proceeded. *"Being, which is covered by the etheric mantle, creates thoughts by Will. And these, by the intention of the Soul, direct themselves in movement, generating energy. When this energy, which emanates from the Soul, is set in motion, it creates the 'explosion of force' called emotion.*

"Emotions in themselves transcend what the Soul is trying to express toward the physical domain. In turn they reflect the

thoughts and thus create an image. The image builds the instrument for action and thus controls behavior."

"Fascinating!" I exclaimed. "Thoughts reflect themselves in images, and thus the astral/imaginative plane is created. Therefore when the Soul speaks to the body, it uses emotion as its language. When it speaks to itself, it uses symbols, shapes and forms. That's why the embrace of the universes was so much like lovers' play. What a fantastic way to bring God down to earth! Loving was the rule in which Life's game was played. How," I asked, "could we have forgotten?"

"By not understanding what the human instrument was," said the Cat.

"Then now," I urged, "is the time to tell me."

"Almost," said the Cat. *"First let's feel ourselves together."*

And as I centered in the Soul, Spirit expanded through the Purple Rose into the Wholeness of the realms. It filled Mind to its finitude, and from here I understood that I was dressed in ethers, and that ether was in Mind, and that Mind was in feeling, and that feeling was in image.

Each quality of Essence was present as a perfect gem—a jewel or a metal—in the crown of Self. And all were perceived through what I called my central eye, the perfect diamond of white light. From this light the Essence of the Soul—I Am—magnified the shining force of the crystal Will, the golden beautiful Love, the healing emerald of Truth, and the ruby, the symbol of strength. It was the blue-pearl light of Wisdom that enabled me to accept the splendor of this spectacular panorama. "How great I Am!" I said and felt and saw and sensed. Yet how little I had known about my Self when I'd lived on third-dimensional Terra (earth), where I'd suppressed feelings of my Self and never thought of the glory of Life. I had believed I was only a body that sensed and felt reactively to what was in my environment. What a limited vision I had had!

"Which you still have, when you relate to Self or body," the Cat interrupted. *"Look at it this way: A car has four wheels, a body has seven. Plus five radars into metacosmic dimensions."*

"I have seen many bodies," I said, "but I never saw any wheels."

"All of history can be understood in terms of the first seven wheels. When those wheels function cleanly, the bodies act as channels for the Soul to voyage through the densities of matter; but when the wheels don't function cleanly, the bodies believe in their automatism and dream that they are independent of the Soul. Let me show you the wheels.

"The seventh one is like a radio; it is in contact with Essence, and all of Life comes in and out through it. It is on the crown, above the head, like a thousand-petaled lotus. The sutures of the skull breathe, and the Spirit breathes itself in at birth or when the Being starts to be of service. Every night during so-called sleep it lets go and voyages to the other planes, leaving the body behind. From there the other five chakras get activated and, according to the individual's work, the radar expands to this solar system, the galaxy, the sun of this universe, the meta-universes or the Great Central Sun. It is in this Great Central Ra where the truest feeling of Spirit's source resides and the whole system is evolving back to its home.

"The sixth wheel is slightly below the seventh. It comes through the diamond — it runs the car and directs its path toward unfoldment. Two lights on each side illuminate the roads; these are called 'eyes.'

"Remember the sound in the midst of the silence, the vibration of Wholeness? This is the fifth wheel, through which Truth can be spoken.

"Yet it is at the fourth where Truth resides. Immunity in its truest sense is in the heart of sacredness; the thymus gland in the body recognizes what is the body's own and what is separate or alien. Here is where humans went astray, functioning widely in the lower end of their wheels, but slightly disconnected from above.

"The three lower wheels allow the Will and Strength and Life to flow, and are in charge of work on the material planes.

"The seeds of the body, animated by the Purple Rose, flow through the middle of the lowest wheels, and the power to move and be on earth resides therein.

"Now," concluded the Cat, *"around this axis is built all that is needed: The brain, like a huge computer, being a transducing energy device for the third dimension, connects it all; the heart*

circulates it; the bones sustain the engine. But mainly what you need to know is that all of this lasts only for awhile."

"Remember the aging, decaying process?" asked Augustus. *"It was placed there for humans to look to that which didn't change. Yet they all forgot. Each wheel comes from a different origin..."*

"...and therefore," said the Cat, *"part of man's work on earth is assembling, alignment and function."*

"Each time a center forgets that it is a channel, it functions only in relation to its own history. For example, let's say the heart forgets that it is here for Truth and therefore for the Soul — that it decides to be a separated self. Then all the loves and hates and sorrows propelled by the feelings are not cleared — on the contrary, they get stuck. Thus the person behaves not as if he is in present time but as if he is stuck back in the reacting to his feelings. When each wheel plays its role independently, everything is stuck in the memory of each wheel."

"Outstanding!" I said. "No wonder the psychiatric theories about the mind made partial sense."

"Indeed," said Augustus, *"very rarely does the mind as such interfere with a human's life. It is mostly the* **incompleteness** *of the partial experience that creates the conflict. Besides, each Soul, through all of its bodies, picks the areas of incompleteness that it desires to know and clear throughout that life. Unfortunately, in the flesh it forgets and* ***it*** *was the one that made the choice."*

"But of course," I said. "How could they have limited the perception to only one life? Yet sometimes they even limited it to one *episode* of one life, paying no attention to the Wholeness of the Self."

"You see," said Androgyny, *"it is forgetting Source that creates all the misunderstandings. But there is no need to judge. It is because of judgments that an incompleteness arises. When the seventh wheel opens, it sees — it doesn't judge. Each time we judge, we empower the causation of that image — when we say that something is ugly, we impress the statement of 'ugly' on the natural beauty. Therefore we see our own judgment, not the Reality that is there in front of us."*

"How complex all this is becoming," I whispered to the

Cat. "It was so simple when I just merged in the Oneness of the All."

"Nonsense," said William. *"It is not complex at all. As a matter of fact, it doesn't even exist right now, since nobody is around to claim it."*

"But didn't you say — or the Cat or someone — that at the same time that it doesn't exist, a new world and the Wholeness of the material plane are being created?"

"Indeed," said the Cat, *"and you and we are instrumental in creating it anew. But before that happens, total integration needs to occur so that you can be ordinarily present and know what's going on."*

I sensed that these episodes had a plot, a plan — almost a humorous one. I'd been shown many incompleted statements and heard many actions suggested. These had enabled me to feel that I had set myself up for a learning that, when embodied and transmitted, could contribute to transform our way of being alive.

In that moment I learned about excitement! I shivered throughout all my fields, and asked myself, "Who am *I* to do this work?

"That question is not proper," replied the Cat. *"Don't ask; obey and integrate. Take the deepest of your breaths, look into the crystal and see. You are not special in this work; it is the work of Life. It is co-creation of Heaven on Earth."*

I inspired deeply and looked at William. He handed me the crystal, and in it I saw Agna, no longer sobbing on the spaceship, but standing in the Wholeness of her Self in the presence of her Will, Beauty and Truth. Now she was learning all that I had learned and was seeing in *her* crystal thousands and thousands of other "I"s in the same situation.

"Kaleidoscopic reflections of reality," said Augustus. *"Know now that all earthlings were tried and tested until this time arises. And in this resurrection time, a new voyage lies ahead. That will be the time of the end of lessons of trial and tribulation and the beginning of the lessons of abundance, prosperity and everlasting Joy."*

The story was so circular that I no longer knew whether I

was still on earth and had dreamt it all or whether it was all true. The story seemed to have repeated itself for many eons. All people on the material planes had their own sagas, yet all were similar: The Big Bang of the start (or was it the end?); the times of Pagan; outer space; the love of Soul; the Oneness of the All; the timeless space; the spaceless time —was it all true, or is it all to come?

Augustus shook me out of my thoughts. *"It's time to complete your learnings and do the practice of Love. You lack an understanding of possession, but you will soon be briefed on that."*

"But from now on," Androgyny added, *"in order to remember, spend more time in total alignment with Spirit, where no time is and space has not been known."*

"Become the Oneness in the silence of the Self," advised Beauty. *"and please always remember Who You Are."*

"Yes," said the Cat, *"always and in all ways. That's the only way we can unite with you. When you forget the qualities of Essence, we have to wait for your remembrance, so we sit in expectancy of your presence."*

"Can't you remind me?" I asked.

They all smiled. *"Relax,"* said Will. *"After the GFH there really is nothing to fear."*

Chapter 13

Resonance

Thus in order for man to become a hu-man Being, the physical instrument needed to be tuned to the cosmic breath. Abram became Abra-ham; Bram became Brahman etc. This tuning represented the original easy experience of resonance — the vibration of a cleared physical instrument in alignment with the other bodies and with the purpose of the Soul Self. Any form of energy interfering with this resonance would delay the process of unity, and all actions derived from these impressions would separate the human race instead of bringing it together. The Soul itself had its own timing, its own rhythms for the learning; and through the qualities of Essence it would create circumstances that seemed difficult to overcome unless the individual realized his original commitment to identify with Self and stay focused on the unfoldment process of his life.

From this point of vision the GFH had been the elimination of the bodies; man had become so alien to himself that he could neither listen nor see, and thus no healing was possible.

Healing — yes! I thought. The only way to really heal was to bring all into alignment with the Self, not to apply the cures we made on earth. Medical sciences had forgotten all notions of resonance, and had functioned mechanically for the last few hundred years of life on earth. Even the basic assumption of the studies was divided in two: "body" versus "mind."

The cutting off of organs — the mutilation of this vehicle when growth occurred — was a common practice, and thus the lords of currency invaded the medical field. Never did it occur to them that excessive growths (cancer) always happened when the resonance of the body was out of alignment. Furthermore, there was total ignorance about the existence of other bodies —

feeling, mental, etheric and the like. If anyone talked about them in theory, he was labeled a storyteller or a philosopher; if anyone talked about them in Truth, he was labeled a mystic; and if anyone *acted* on his vision, he was in danger (so scared of Truth had people become) of being locked up in dissidents' housing (prisons and hospitals) so that the prevailing system of ignorance would not be threatened.

As the energies of life were suppressed, body growth or wild imaginings arose, ran out of control and developed into energies to be feared. Spiritual choices were overshadowed by physical, emotional or mental states, and agreements and vows were made to support only those states.

Thus humans were completely alienated from their divine Self. We all know the actions that took place—avoidance of each other, forgetfulness of how the Self is mirrored in bodies, and bizarrely "normal" behaviors to defend the alter ego. People restricted their notion of Self to the survival of the viewpoint from a body that was locked into a crystallized form. That was the normal way of life.

As the discernment of Truth was lost, it was replaced by the knowledge of right and wrong. "Right" was whatever was in accordance with the prevailing viewpoint; "wrong" was anything that disagreed. Later a legal system formed in which the rules of those in power again took precedence over the survival of the race.

Fourth-dimensional disincarnated people—or even sometimes points of view (which were feelings or thoughts in magnetic form)—created patterns of reflection in the astral plane, from where they held onto earth and to their view of right and wrong. They no longer had access to the material world, but in the form of entities they still had control over the making of the worlds. In fact, they had such an influence that whole populations behaved according to their wishes.

Human beings prayed (consciously or unconsciously) to these astral forms, and thus became servants of their own imagination. They acted like Soulless creatures and functioned as humanoid robots, relinquishing not only all responsibility for themselves, but also all interest in finding out who they were and what their Source was. They believed that they were made of flesh, that somewhere they had a Soul, and that there were ways to find the Soul (but usually this was thought to happen only after the death of the body, and then only if people behaved in the manner prescribed by the astral-image forms). These patterns later were locked into cults, and a few dominated the masses.

These forms of life — these Imagos — that became a thick layer on the astral plane were rebellious souls without bodies. They controlled the ruling of the earth, and all the attempts of Soul messengers who had, over time, come to teach people about regaining their freedom were quickly converted into mere adoration of Imagos. This was the highest level that the human mind could conceive.

Religions, philosophies and valued teachers were thus crystallized into an image formed by the minds of men on earth; and as the followers nourished this image, they too became disconnected from their Truth. All qualities of Essence — the emerald, the ruby, the diamond, and so on — had become symbols of something of past value only, to be collected or hoarded. Jewels had no reference to the substantial value in the Self, merely to the sparkling, expensive, material manifestation. Love — the vital cohesiveness of Souls — was regarded as just "a feeling"; populations measured their satisfaction by the feelings that possessed them, and finally by the objects that they had acquired. Ultimately, it was things, inanimate objects, that determined who they were. Sciences and learning institutions devoted themselves to classifying bodies according to what the bodies liked, how they felt, what they owned, how they related or what they did. Thus the nature of man was defined in terms of these variables, this psychosociocultural identity.

The energy of the feeling plane, locked into the astral-physical conjunction, fixated each human born on earth into forgetting his origin; and the fear of lying about the Self (including such intermediate forms of lying as pride or lust or anger) had converted Love into unhealthy forms of relating. Thus, clashing bodies tried to change each other through wars, never conceiving that the only change possible was to expand into and include the Whole.

So although Pagan, the Red Patriarchs, and the Navigating Pastor all seemed to disagree in words, they all were working for the same thing – different expressions of Imagos. Whether they called it "right" or "left," "war" or "peace," humanoids were totally indifferent about each other.

"Such," concluded Augustus, *"was the state of affairs close to the final countdown, at the end of the second millennia of some era."*

"Augustus," I said, "thank you for empowering me with your straight description. Did Imago know what was taking place?"

"Yes. On earth there is autonomy. From a Soul's point of vision, the etheric, mental and feeling bodies are robes or garments of the Self. When the Soul voyages, forgetting takes place and people concentrate their functioning solely through matter. But the purpose of life on earth is wholly to integrate the Whole and to function as a Soul on earth – learning and returning at will. So autonomy also means integrated functioning with Will."

I recalled the purpose of the Council of Twelve: Before the first cosmic war, Beings had lived in harmony – but in a harmony like that of a colony of corals. So the war was created to individuate each Being throughout the universe to a full awareness of the Soul. The Lords of Darkness were therefore only less enlightened angels. They were not evil, as they themselves projected thought forms in the mental realms. No one realized that they were working as obstacles for enlightenment only to strengthen all into the joy of Ascension. War also ultimately served the universal peace plan.

"When humans discarded their vehicles and finally realized this," Augustus continued, *"they asked the same question we told you not to ask: 'Who am I to be shown the resonance of All?' This question creates separation in the frequency of isolation, thus blocking the brain from perceiving the cosmic Whole."*

Hosts of fifth-dimensionally aware Masters began to descend and embody divine attributes at the end of times in order to cause the fulfillment of the morphic resonance plan.

While I had been asking why I was so different and so special, others were being taught the same thing!

"That arrogant question," the Cat added, *"creates pride and fixates the alter ego in isolation. So man-without-a-body shifted his awareness to his image, which 'flew' through the astral worlds and became the Imago of himself, behaving autonomously and controlling bodies through its thoughts. Thus man cut himself off from the higher planes; and the higher five wheels, though fully operating, became functional only during deep sleep or profound meditations."*

"But," interrupted Androgynous, *"this behavior was not really autonomous — in the astral plane these entities have no notion of the Soul."*

"Exactly!" the Cat concluded.

"Of course!" I said. "How can an overcoat have any notion of its owner?"

"It can't," replied the Cat. *"That is why life on the material plane has looked as it has for years. But the 'overcoat' can control to the extent that it gets wet in its journey. On earth this process was called 'negative motivation,' and it called forth a creative process called 'destruction.' That's what you saw on earth. The lack of Soul nourishment negatively motivated man to blow himself up into oblivion."*

"Yes!" I exclaimed, remembering Pagan. He had felt so committed to his work — had he known he was really a puppet of Imago? Some people who had been under Imago's influence finally realized their vanity after a breakdown in their lives; others collapsed fully and disappeared. Serving Twilight Masters was ultimately useless. In the end, all collapsed and disappeared. That is how they all banned authenticity from their lives. Authenticity was public enemy number one, by all these forms. Churchianity burned authentics; others shot them, drugged them, sliced their bodies into pieces or confined them.

"Authenticity!" I declared. "Come present before me!" And the silver sword of Authenticity manifested before me, turning into a strong, beautiful Being.

"I am that," it said, *"which, even in the darkest of nights, is present through all worlds. When Beauty is forgotten, I take its form; when Truth is displaced, I become it. When Strength is gone,*

I am it; when Wisdom sleeps, I am awake. I Am here to serve, because I am you. I am One with you. I used to come to you in dreams as the words of conscience, in speech in the manner of ethics, in lies in the slipping of the Truth. In falseness I reflected on your face. I lived in the hearts of men up to the last moment, and brought forward another quality, which you now need to know."

Stardust then appeared, and a voice came forth like a rain of stars: *"I am Forgiveness. I am the ultimate action of Love. After errors are made, I give as before. I don't condemn others nor my Self, and I understand all acts with the nature of true Love. And I forgive you also for the doubts that you have had in your Self. I remind you that those doubts came only when you forgot the court over which you preside. I unlock for you the presence of this quality of Essence. Creativity, come forth!"*

A beautiful woman with a halo of yellow light came present in my etheric robe. *"I have always been here for you to call upon,"* she said. *"Call upon me and I will manifest."*

"Indeed," said William, *"we are a team."* And as these new qualities of Essence started to appear, I experienced the quiet release of surprise.

Then orange Joy came onto the scene smiling. I acknowledged her and welcomed the stream of attributes in my field that were Being. I understood why some Muslims on earth had said that peace shall come when all the names of God — all the attributes of Essence — shall sing together.

I was learning what Cat had promised I would learn — the science of peace and the shattering of ignorant veils before my journey toward — what? The adventure of my life presented the next vision on my road. Where this journey was to unfold I did not know, but faith held me in its arms so I could go on.

I was content.

Yet I knew surprises were to come.

Chapter 14

Here We Go

Before the GFH, the humanoids had thought of earth as a planet in which life occurred in an isolated form. People and animals were thought to be alive, but other forms were thought to be inanimate. And earth was thought to be the only place that had "intelligent" life — life on other planets or dimensions of the universe were "fictitious."

According to this human, planet-centered way of being, the consciousness of scarcity prevailed and the fight for survival ended up being the most common way of living. At the end of the Age of Pagan this notion had invaded all aspects of human life; thus families disintegrated and men and women coupled not from Self but from body/ego-centered activities of the flesh. These asserted themselves under various flags of "liberation" — and each "liberated" form and lifestyle competed with the next. Behavior was controlled from the astral plane by entities, thought forms and lesser energies, and inner as well as outer violence broke the structures of life.

In the midst of this corruption of matter, some illustrious Beings came to earth to help man know the Self. They were called the Navigators, and they taught about what is beyond the physical form. Each community that attracted a Navigator was blessed. They taught different ways of living as a way to break Imago's forms.

Meditation was the most widespread teaching. It enabled humans to focus thoughts and, through their breath, to transcend the limits of the bodily form. But the more communities opened to the force of Light, the more that unenlightened humanoids tried to suppress such communities. Few people could really reap the benefits of the work.

Lakshmi was one such person. Throughout her lives she had learned to know the Truth; and through this Truth she lived at peace. She was young but wise, and in her body she carried the seeds of cosmic Life.

As I was looking into the crystal of my Will, I saw Lakshmi playing, caressing animals, watering plants and picking flowers. I sensed her Beauty, and her Light was enormous. She was wealthy in her qualities of Essence. Her imagination was not a path to delusion, but instead a tool for her creation; her feelings carried only the beauty of her thoughts. She had known, before the GFH, that it didn't matter whether her life on that planet continued or not; she trusted fully in the love of God, and every day in her prayers and absolutions, she knew divine Will was done.

As Lakshmi's body came into maturity, her heart was pure: Sensuality flowed from her skin, yet there was no lust. She was so beautiful, so full of Self, so loving, that I spent hours absorbed in the crystal, looking at her. Yet although I felt, saw and sensed all her essential qualities, I couldn't see her face.

She knew that GHF would lead to one of the two resolutions of all astral planets. It would become a star radiating Light either because of mass illumination through the implosion of consciousness into the particle of Truth or because of mass explosion. Such is the nuclear risk. From a distance all turned into Light. The rhythm of the universe was ever expanding, and as such there was really only one way to go.

"Help me, Cat!" I requested; but nothing could be done. And Androgynous couldn't see her, either.

I went to my pearl for Wisdom and it said: *"As you learn to recognize the qualities of Self, you will find them in Lakshmi."*

But I wanted to meet her. Day by day I longed for such a precious friend. Despite the vastness of my Self and the knowledge of Life, I still longed for company. This company had to become the value of my life. I cried, and as the tears fell they crystallized in lakes.

But I still couldn't see her face. I begged and wept and laughed; but Lakshmi remained the same.

"Augustus, wisdom!" I cried.

And he said, *"This longing – this drive that is taking place – is the fuel of love. It will enable you to merge with us when it is time for your navigator work."*

"Now," the Purple Rose exclaimed, *"just see how Love kindles the Soul, which moves the static into the eternal motion of life."*

"Meditation is one way of centering the gravity of the material world," said Compassion. *"When you are in that place, you may experience a certain knowledge, an attribute of my Soul – you feel for others, and the love of Self moves on into another Self. It is lack of Compassion that deteriorated human beings; they accused each other of caring more about themselves than about others, but the Truth is that it's* **when** *you care about your Self that you care for all others."*

How different this was from what I'd felt in my last life on earth! There I had lived like a stone, had learned to contain myself, had set limits to my Self. I'd never known this before, and I now experienced true rage because of it.

"Wonderful!" exclaimed Augustus. *"That is what taught you humility. That is why you are here now. You see, humanoids appreciated only what they thought they 'liked,' and by limiting themselves to only that narrow form of appreciation, they contracted their way of life. 'Good or bad,' 'right or wrong,' 'positive or negative' – these dualities (which were reflections of Imago) ruled their lives. Your experience as a living stone was neither bad nor good – while you did contain your true Self, you also healed the wounds of thought. And thus you became free from all lives in the wheels of your vehicle, which enabled you to free yourself today."*

"Oh!" I said, "you mean stabilization of consciousness."

"Exactly," Compassion replied. *"Stabilization of the Self, which can be achieved only in the material plane. How this takes place is the choice of each person's history."*

"But," I argued, remembering my most recent sufferings, "the being I was on earth was so brutal – there was no space for Love!"

"Not so," said Augustus. *"Remember that it enabled you to feel Compassion, without which you could never feel the Love you feel for Lakshmi."*

"But I thought everyone was now receiving the same lessons as myself, after the GFH."

"Yes — everyone who completed their life on earth."

"How did they do that?"

"By being all that one can be on earth — the best, the worst, the good, the bad, and all those definitions of the mind."

I thanked Compassion for her service in my life, and released my thoughts into the cosmic void.

"How long did the suffering go on?" asked Androgynous.

"Till I said STOP!" And so saying, I looked into the crystal. This time I saw all those beings who had not completed earth. They returned to worlds similar to earth to continue their cycle of selves. Others went into the astral, feeling or mental zones, and a few of them into etheric realms. But all the others in the Soul were here in the fifth dimension and above, enjoying the Wholeness of the Self.

"So really," said the Cat, *"nothing got worked out by blowing the planet up. But a lot of tears were shed."*

"Look," said Will, *"Pagan is now doing the same thing once again on that earth right down the Milky Way."*

"And the Reds with him," I said, looking. "It looks like space-time's eternal machine repeats itself — but I'd like to know what I am doing here."

All the essential qualities, attuned, said together, *"You are to start a brand-new race. We thought you'd never ask! As soon as you are trained in Life, we'll go."*

I thought of Agna, excited by lust; I thought of another — from the past? Or was it the future ecstatic joining of the Selves — Bhakti-Shadai, with her sweet, heartfelt kisses. The two thoughts balanced each other, and I remained on neutral.

The feeling of Lakshmi was back, and thus I learned what Hope was:

A world of peace
a world of love
a city of gold
the stars above.

There was a melody to go with these words, and I expanded myself wide and open into the wings of universal Love. I whirled and whirled around, merging once again into the Wholeness of the Soul.

Great peace
Great breath,
the clarity of purpose
seemed true
this time
seemed true.

I saw a world of Love and shouted to the circle. Certainty came into my system, which now was once again the Wholeness of my bodies, and it felt as if breath started entering the physical instrument.

"Yes, insufflation. That is the true meditation. It is hard to teach it just by activating the body. It is the whole Spirit, your Holy Spirit, that must be in charge to move the empire fully," said one of the voices.

It seemed like trying to start a new car. But this time the car was fully conscious.

It was the chariot of the Self.

The activation of the wheels excited my Self, and I knew a great adventure was about to start.

In the fullness of the One, I was complete. Yet I did not know why the eventual encounter with Lakshmi was exciting me so much. It was my aliveness and her aliveness that would start me off on my next episode of life.

I clearly felt I had a mission to perform. And for this mission I had been given Wisdom, Beauty, Light, and Will; I was immersed in the fragrance of the Purple Rose, which held the emerald of Truth in the witnessing of Authenticity, Compassion, Forgiveness, and the other qualities of Essence; and I wore my robes of force and churned the wheels of this vehicle, so similar to my body but now en-Lightened.

I knew that although old pictures of earth were gone and totally destroyed, there were myriads of similar worlds with similar people through whom to enliven the Soul of Self. It was now clear: People didn't have a Soul, but Soul had a people. The work to do could not be like any done before, yet the vessels were alike.

So excited and full of life was I that I didn't notice the disappearance of the stars, the suns, and the moons.

"Hyperspace again," said Cat. *"I wonder where we'll land."*

Part II

ON TRIA RA

Chapter 1

Boy Is Born

Said Lakshmi to Arcanus, "I love you so much. This night with you, beloved husband, has been heavenly."

"Dear one," replied Arcanus, "I feel that tonight we have conceived a child."

"I hope so — I've waited for you for thousands of years! You are to be what the sun is to the earth."

"And you to me, dear wife, mate of my soul. I love you, I love you, I love you!"

~ ❧ ~

As these bodies thrashed together — as Arcanus' sperm penetrated Lakshmi's ovum — I realized that from the fifth dimension I began to take responsibility for the creation of my third-dimensional physical body. I never expected to begin the whole cycle again — but of course, there is no shortcut for entering matter!

"Oh yes, there is," said the Cat, *"you could walk in instead of the usual crawl in, but then a learning period would be different from the one you are about to have!"*

I recognized Lakshmi from those other times, when I had fallen in love with her essential qualities but had not been able to see her face. Now I would see it — and the face would be the face of what I would call "my" mother. I was ready to enter the traditional nine-month cycle of events in order to become human on Tria Ra, a place that greatly resembled earth in form, energy level and behavior. Yet I was three million light years away from the late Terra GFH planet.

I recorded each encounter between my parents within my

Self, and by the end of the nine months I could have written a book! The wheels of my newly-in-creation body registered stress, neglect, ecstasy, pain, joy, unconsciousness and delight in multisensorial ways. I received the imprint of smells, sounds, sights — not only in each successive moment but also for the entire sequence of circumstances — and I fully understood that it was only because of the Spirit that I was and because I was protected by essential qualities that I did not forget myself.

Other babies typically forgot who they were, identifying with their body's shock-absorptions completely. By the time the liquid of the gentle, aqueous container, the womb, was loosed, this body already had a history of circumstances. This history was generally so marked by image and emotion that, once born, babies would not know their Selves and would struggle for the rest of their lives whenever these in-utero circumstances were restimulated. (These struggles they would see not as mere restimulation, but as a matter of survival.) Every event would be so uniquely imprinted that any time in life a circumstance would evoke it, a dreamy state of unconsciousness would fall on the being's notion of Self and a stress-related artillery would be set in motion to preserve survival. Therefore, only about one baby on any plane of matter was born pure.

As far as I could see, considering the vehicle I would be navigating in, that baby would not be me.

~ ❧ ~

Boom, boom, boom! Lakshmi's heartbeat grew intense. And as the contractions started to press against my body, I lost all sense of balance. Amazing! I thought, calling forth the virtue of tolerant endurance as I was propelled through a tunnel. I could perceive a light at its end, while being shaken rapidly in all directions. My head bounced against the walls of this canal, and every cell of this new system I was about to use knew deeply the effects of pressure.

No wonder reincarnated entities had an issue with freedom! At such an early stage does the body learn the entrapment of matter. I could easily have forgotten my Self, if not for my guardian angel, the Purple Rose. As my body came out of

Lakshmi's, the Purple Rose insufflated me with Spirit, and from my body emerged a strange, painful noise: "Wa-a-a!" I screamed, feeling the pressure of the exchange of liquids for air. Arcanus joyfully embraced my mother: "It's a boy, it's a boy!"

From then on I was called Boy. I had a new identity for now, and whoever referred to me called me such.

Suddenly, the only hose that pumped for this newly created entity was cut off harshly, leaving me on my own. No one cared to see how I was doing as the umbilical cord was cut.

I looked at the face of Lakshmi for the first time. Her big eyes looked back with so much love that it triggered my memory of all I had felt for her. Soulmate, I thought, don't you remember me?

"He looks just like you," she said to Arcanus. Thus came the first blow to my individuation. How stupid can she be? I wondered. Not only did she not see my Self, but above all how could a newborn boy be like this big old man? At any rate, how can any One look like any other One? What a lack of respect was present on this planet! But it had looked so cool from the other dimensions...

She placed me against her breast, and a white viscous substance of the liquid state flowed down my throat. I started coughing.

"He sucks, he sucks, how wonderful," she screamed, almost causing a blow in my tympanic membrane. "And he loves my milk," she added.

What a reception in this new matter state, I thought. I was tempted to go to sleep, forget my Self, and go through the motions of human life, convinced that everything that begins must end and that time was only relative. But Augustus reminded me of Who I Was and what I was here to learn.

"But it's like going back to grade one," I complained.

"No," said he, *"grade zero! Always remember the Wholeness. Closed circle!"*

I reflected on my past precious episode on earth and, having just passed through these few moments in a body, forgave everyone. I had judged the Age of Pagan; I had fought, screamed and judged again; but now I saw that this existence in the material world actually encouraged babies to leave upon arrival — forgetting Self, forgetting about learning to Be, and lying about the Source of Life. They thought it was the parents' fault. But the problem was material existence itself. It is called "entering boot camp," and the main goal was to keep Purpose alive till recruitment time would come again. Instant forgiveness overcame me, and the Presence of Compassion was so strong that I dropped some tears.

"The baby is crying," said my dad. *"He must be hungry."* And the breast was in my mouth again.

Don't they ask here what the Being wants? I thought. Cat, at my side, was laughing. *"Now the qualities of Essence get to become real,"* it said. *"Now the adventure begins."*

Chapter 2

First Birthday

Why I had to be born again into an earth-type existence was a mystery to me, and I couldn't even ask my parents about it. During my few months in this physical instrument, "Boy" had not yet learned to articulate language. Certainly, Lakshmi, Arcanus and I all understood the language of the Soul; but the Soul was veiled so deeply from their awareness that they thought the wholeness of their Selves was reflected in what was called "just normal good people," with their bad and good moments, behaviors and thoughts. Typical third-dimensional standards.

~ ❧ ~

It was the first-year birthday of my body. Mom and dad, aunts and uncles, cousins and friends gathered around a big table, pinched my cheeks and celebrated how big "I" was. Little did they know about my real size, let alone Who and What I Was; nevertheless a lot of joy went on in celebrating my body shape. Lakshmi and Arcanus were filled with pride. They themselves were nice people. Lakshmi was not really behaving like the Lakshmi I had seen on the level of her Soul.

What am I doing at this table? I asked myself as I looked into everybody's eyes, searching for someone real and conscious of them Selves. My gaze rested on an older man. His eyes were blue, and through his wrinkled face I could perceive a loving smile. As we looked into each other's eyes, his Spirit spoke to me: "I am he who is called L-yon, and in Tria Ra I have been Lakshmi's father. That makes me your grandfather. I am what is known to be an old man and I have come here to give you a birthday gift."

Another gift, I thought disappointedly, looking at the teddy bears, balls, rabbits, tiny clothes and shoes spread out on the sofa — another gift!

"Yes — the gift of devotion," L-yon answered.

I asked, "Devotion — what does that look like?"

"It looks," he replied, "like the calmness of my eyes with light shining through. Like the silence of my smile. Like the harmony in my heart, like reaching old age on this plane in health and peace. Above all, for me it looks like the practice of prayer to my Lord three times a day, despite rain or heat or snow."

"Prayer." The word struck me as something old and familiar. "Do you mean asking your Lord for something?"

"No," he said. "That is the way bodies pray. The Soul praises, through commitments, the grandness of its Spirit. And to balance the arrogance of knowing, calls it God, Spirit at its Greatness."

"God," I responded. "Of course! The cycles of infinite universal Generation, Operation and Destruction; justly and mercifully succeeded by Grant, Order and Direct Beingness."

"Yes, but here it's been made external in forms, so those who do not know the Wholeness do not become arrogant in themselves." Hearing the word "arrogance" twice, I requested more knowledge. But the partying interrupted our conversation.

"We will sing happy birthday to him now!" said Dad, as Mother put a new kind of food, with two candles, in front of me.

"One candle for now and one for the year to come." Enlightenment for the future, I pondered. Meanwhile, the confined energy of sounds came from the others, who were simply going through obligatory rituals and motions. They really cared little for me, and that was perfectly all right with me — but definitely unenlightened for them.

"You know," said one of my aunts, "it's a pity that he can't enjoy this beautiful birthday party — he is so little and all his feelings are so underdeveloped that he can't know."

Nonsense! I reacted silently. She is not even aware of the presence of her feeling body; therefore all this is just words to her.

Whereupon Compassion entered the room and said, *"Lesson number one on this birthday is to have me present when you see and hear like that."*

"This poor woman," added Forgiveness, *"is to be forgiven instantly for not knowing what she does."*

L-yon looked into my eyes and nodded: "This is arrogance —what you have done and what she has done. Without knowing, she speaks as if she knew about you and your feelings and Self. Then you —without Compassion (that is, forgetting your loving knowledge of the Oneness of All and your Self) —judge her in turn. Even though you thought you knew that the God you praised was the God of her opinion, since this contrasted with your Self-awareness, you then evaluated her expression as false. Little devotion," added L-yon, "to the truth."

"And that," he said aloud, "is why your granddaddy is here." And he kissed my cheeks and thus became part of the celebrating act. I remembered how on earth Native Americans called the Lord "Grandpa Great Spirit" —how handy his intervention at this time!

~ ❧ ~

Funny evening, I thought as I was being undressed and put to bed. Meanwhile, the guests gathered in the living room to talk, smoke and chit-chat. Since it was already sunset, L-yon excused himself and went into another room to pray.

I left my body lying on my bed and went to watch, astro-projecting my Self. He was so absorbed in his prayer that he didn't notice me. I saw his path —it was called religion. It was based on 613 laws, some of them similar to the old Ten Commandments that people didn't follow on earth, and also to others that were more complex. His family thought he was imprisoned by religion. In a way he was, but not in the way they thought. Some prisons are homes for a time and similarly some homes are prisons. To him it was definitely a launching base for his survival on this plane.

In the border territory between the etheric and the Soul, a cosmic mirror reflects all. When Beings, in their process of enlightenment, catch a glimpse of their Spirit and call it the Lord, they think it is them Selves. (This is true when they look from above the mirror, but when they look from below, it is only a reflection.)

Thus many Masters see their reflection in this mirror; then, without expanding their identity to encompass their third- and fifth-dimensional DNA, they return to their genetic entity; and when they are back in the body, they establish rules and guidelines to be followed. These become the pattern of religion. The elevated man, as L-yon had often told me, knows that these forms exist to contain the teaching – but sometimes religions see the form as higher than the goal.

"The physical body needs to conform," said L-yon at the end of his prayer, noticing my presence. "If not, it falls apart. Devotion is a way to give it form." And he showed me how to pray.

I looked back at my bed where my body was lying and listened to its breath. With each breath the body was doing a very familiar and natural prayer. (Later I found out that this was called "meditation" and that there were expert teachers all around Tria Ra teaching "mantras" to people to help them connect with their breath.)

Through the breath the body was constantly reminding itself, "I am, I am, I am, I am, Haiam, Haiam, Haiam." And as the name was constantly repeated, I adopted it as mine: HAIAM.

So it was that on the evening of my first birthday celebration, I heard the right name for my body. As I became aware of this the body relaxed even deeper, and L-yon came into the room, as if aware of what had taken place. "Blessed are you, Lord of the Universe," he said, "who has now connected this body to this Soul." Thus he made a commitment to guide it for nine years.

Through the open door came mother, father and some guests to see "the angel" rest. Little did they know how true their statement was. My body turned around and cried, disturbed by the light filtering through the door.

"Let him sleep," they all agreed, unaware that while my body rested, I was in total vigilance.

"The Soul never sleeps," L-yon said.

"Oh, you always have to bring God into the conversation," complained his oldest son, a "scientist," who believed only what had been tested, demonstrated, proven and produced.

"No, my son," L-yon said humbly, "it is always Spirit who allows the conversations to be brought forth."

~ ❧ ~

"Isn't it time to have another child?" asked Arcanus as he joined with Mother.

"I don't know, but I have a feeling Spirit does," she replied, climaxing in ecstatic joy.

Chapter 3

School

"Goodness gracious," said the frog, "this woman is pregnant again!" Lakshmi was showing signs of growth in her abdomen.

"What?" I said, "Now I can hear frogs talk? And I still can't speak to people. What do you mean, 'pregnant'?"

"I represent fertility," said the frog. "You are going to have a brother or sister."

I looked at Lakshmi. Inside her the embryonic differentiation had not yet begun; yet certainly enough, Amada — my sister-to-become — was already there. From inside the womb she was carefully energizing every action. The chromosomes in her DNA in my mother's uterus were activated — as are all biochemical changes — according to the patterns of the Soul. Amada was an ancient Soul with knowledge of herself. She had chosen to come down to help me learn and support our Mission. My future little sister was going to be my master. This would be her first assignment in matter.

As mother's pregnancy progressed, Amada and I established a relationship. She let me in on her secret: She would not be coming through the birth canal, because she did not want to expose the tiny baby body to the harshness of compression. Thus she produced some small hemorrhages in my mother's womb, so that at the time of delivery her birth would be totally decompressive, which would diminish the memory of birth stress.

Caesarean sections were obstetrically attributed to all kinds of understandable reasons and conscious excuses. No one ever considered a possible origin in the guidance of Spirit and its choice.

Because my parents did not remember that this baby's Essence was *Beloved,* they named her Linda because she was pretty. Because this was her first assignment in matter, her learning was very hard at first. I, being no longer a baby, would take full charge of her; and she, in the antiquity of her Soul, would show me how to teach her.

"An interesting deal," said L-yon. To me, my grandpa was a guardian angel. So was my sister — and I to her.

Aren't we all?

And so my mother had been, before my incarnation. Now she treated me only as her "son"; she had covered up her Soul too well — I could barely see it. Nor could she.

As for my father (who, interestingly enough, did hold the experience of his Source in his Essence), he was entrapped into surviving in this world, which, as on earth, had no room for spiritual awareness. Again we were immersed as on earth in a male-dominant civilization in which the essence of the androgynous nature was covered up and male bodies were believed to be the sole providers, with values of mental and physical dominance installed in their left-brain apparatus. Logic, strength, linearity, coherence were values that overshadowed receptivity, sensitivity and intuitive knowing even in female bodies who were trying to be as masculinely accepted as their gender counterparts.

It was on my sister's first birthday that L-yon told me about the circular notion of the teaching: In my relationship with Amada there was neither teacher nor student. I was teaching her to walk; she was teaching me to teach her to walk. She was also learning to walk as well as learning to teach me how to teach. Thus each of us was both teaching and learning. This made me inquire: "Grandpa, do you make the prayer or does the prayer make you?"

"Indeed, this is a serious question," L-yon replied. "And for this kind of question you deserve a truthful answer: All is made by Spirit of God. We all make one another. This is a process of co-creation, and this is how the whole universe holographically organizes itself, accommodating all perspectives simultaneously," he added.

~ ❧ ~

It seemed as if life on Tria Ra was as inconsistent as anywhere else in matter. Timelessness was only a notion; birthday after birthday showed the impact of the year.

My parents were getting bored. Lakshmi longed for some romance; Arcanus came home concerned about his dealings of the day. Life looked dull. If not for my sister and Grandpa I would have spent most of my time absorbed in the Essences of my Soul.

One day the Cat made itself present. *"Soon you will enter school,"* he reminded me.

"Not again!" I responded at first, remembering what it had been like on earth.

"You'll like it there," the Cat replied. *"The tasks are new, and you might learn to find the Soul in some of your friends."*

School did not appeal to me. Seeing the mental conditioning of my family, I had learned to be manipulated and to manipulate via tokens of love. "Be a good boy," Dad used to say, "and you'll be able to watch TV till late." "Give me a hug," said Uncle Richard, "and you can have a piece of cookie." They treated me like I was a piece of cookie — slapping me (lovingly), pushing me (jokingly), grabbing me (tearingly) and laughing at or with me. Such a strange, negative love I was immersed in! Even though I had learned the language of the Soul, on Tria Ra it was only the language of emotions that caused anything to happen. Mother made the meals Dad wanted as long as he did the dishes — all in the name of "exchange." But the exchange was based on covert emotional blackmail, which drove their feelings underground. Continuing day after day, this suppressed their aliveness and kept them from being fully happy. All I could do was spend many hours a day in prayer to L-yon's Lord God of the Universe in order to extricate myself and remember who I was. In this context, school was not appealing.

~ ❧ ~

When the first day of school came, I entered without ever looking back. My mother was astonished that I could break the ties so quickly. I loved her more than she was capable of seeing (because she did not love herself enough); but now the focus was school. And being a fully conscious multidimensional entity, at least inside my inner knowing, detachment was easy for me.

Actually all children were alike, trying hard to demonstrate that they were clinging to each other.

All the scared children gathered together while a scared teacher, who herself was still a child, tried to indoctrinate us with letters and numbers.

The symbols made no sense at all. They were called "letters" and later "words" and "sentences." I wasn't too interested, since I could easily read their auric fields, which enabled me to know what was on the blackboard. Amazingly enough, that was also how most of the children knew things. Yet teachers did not reward glancing at wholenesses and knowing the essence of the communications they were trying to teach us. Instead they created punishments for "guessing" and fed bits of information to our little brains (as they liked to named them). Of course, kids were complacent enough to adapt to this terminology, thus adopting smallness as the way of knowing. Many of them gave up the awareness of them Selves in order to relate according to the rules and regulations of the class.

I decided to play fair, and started to learn the words rather than just understanding them aurically. To justify myself, I created a purpose: Amada might need help next year, and I might be of service. Encouraged by this thought, I partially blocked my ability to see auras.

Augustus said, *"Needless sacrifice, my friend. Now it is time to devote yourself, as your grandpa has been teaching you for years."*

And suddenly I saw the value of prayer. Devotion was also *concentration* — and concentration could be used to focus into materiality and from there manage the learning of current realities and their trappings.

Androgynous interrupted: *"You know that you're here to*

learn without using your powers. It is not ethical to intrude into another's private realm unless you are so requested."

"But how can they request help if they don't even *know* they have an auric field?"

Amada replied, "Do you remember how we communicated before I had a body?"

"Yes," I answered, "Soul to Soul."

"So why not do this with others?"

"They don't know they *have* a Soul, so how can they respond?"

"Well, *you* know. Talk to the Soul silently, and with your lips say only what's needed. "Silently love them, bless them and exalt them in the sovereignty and magnificence that they are."

"That sounds like what they call 'a split relationship.'"

"So, Haiam," joked L-yon, "since when are you concerned about what they call things? Haven't you seen how your grandpa gets around?"

"But everybody in the family thinks you are weird," I said. Then, "Oh, sorry, Grandpa," I apologized. "But really, they think you are just a religious freak."

L-yon laughed. "Have their thoughts ever touched their love, or my love for them? I give them room to talk, but when I speak, I speak to Soul."

"You ***are*** *a Soul,"* said Beauty to me. *"But now it's time to reside in it in your relations with school."* Simultaneous learning once again—not only did I have to learn the symbols and meaning of the minds, but I also had to relate to each person as my Self, and to discover in them their Truth.

"A catalyst," I said. "That is what I am."

"That is what ***all*** *life is,"* said Certainty.

"But I don't *want* to manipulate them from their Soul," I protested.

"You couldn't," answered Certainty. *"It is their Soul that begs you to be your Self. Thus they become them Selves. From this day on, expect nothing from this world. You can only give to it; it can only take. There is nothing here that you will need."*

"Oh my," I said, "so it's either being manipulated by *negative love* and doing things its way, or being manipulated by *Love* and doing things its way. What's *my* way?

The Way of Love

The way of love,
that is my way.
I do not fear;
It always is and was.

A sound of silence,
I give away
myself, my heart.
The way it truly is
is upside down.
The way they say it is, is not —
and yet reflection
means the same,
and yet is not.

I love the love of love
and love the strokes of warmth.
I walk a road that leads to me,
where Self and I are merged.

The only form to really Be
is flowing to a love of thee,
is flowing from a hope of thine
into eternity.

Divine illusion is this world,
forbidden fruit of life.
It takes the courage to just Be
And merge the travel line.

A time of strength, of loving force,
which goes from head to earth,
can only bloom in divine grace,
and Lord and I do merge.

Chapter 4

Arcanus Is Healed

Silently I set out to discover Arcanus — his amazing vastness and richness. My father's Soul was disconnected from his conscious awareness by a blockage in the third wheel of his vehicle — in this as well as other lifetimes, his need to have power and control over his environment (of which, he believed, he was the sole cause) had made him block his sensitivity to the upper wheels. Nevertheless, he had attracted my mother as his mate. The beauty of Lakshmi's Soul was always in his etheric field.

Because my father did not know how to digest life, his digestive-pancreatic apparatus was blocked, causing a stomach ulcer. Thus he needed to stay home for weeks, and this provided me with a gracious opportunity for my research. I was allowed to stay with my father for only limited periods, but this was long enough to establish a clear, ongoing communication with his Soul. Thus I learned of all its lifetimes and experiences, since his Soul (like all Souls) keeps the files of everything forever. I discovered that my dad's main attribute of Essence was *Cosmic Memory* — thus his name, Arcanus. Arcanus was the archivist of all akashic records (the files of the universe). In this capacity he had misused his power by revealing this information to lower-level psychics down on earth. They had used it to take over the control of bodies, thus preventing autonomy and promoting dissension, war and injury to the family.

Because he had revealed these records, his Soul was veiled, and he had to earn a living to support his family. However, the time of his submission to conditioning was done, and I was instrumental in bringing about this closure.

It happened like this: One day when I was six and he was

acting pained and irritable, I asked him, "What is our relationship?"

"Obviously, it is merely physical," he replied. "I am your father; you are my child."

"That is why you ache," I said, and walked away.

"Boy, Boy, come back!" he screamed. But I went off to school.

"This child is very disobedient," sputtered Arcanus. "He needs a reprimand! I am sick, and I called him and he didn't respond."

Amada had been watching the scene shyly from a corner of the room. So ethereal that she rarely spoke much, she still spent most of her time on other dimensions and was fairly unaffected by the circumstances of daily life. She never argued or complained. People on this plane hardly realized that silence, sleep or meditation is not inaction, but deep action on many other domains of consciousness. So my parents often took her to doctors, who found nothing wrong with her.

Now, watching Arcanus' reaction, she approached him in a rather unusual way. "Dad," she said, "no one has *just* a physical relation. I rarely speak to you because you seem so engrossed with your work and actions and so burdened by your life. But now that you are sick and vulnerable, we all have come close to you to help you see we love you."

"Of course, of course," he answered, ignoring the words. "I love you also."

"No, you don't!" Amada replied in a voice so firm and powerful that it brought Lakshmi into the room.

"What's going on here?" she asked breathlessly.

"I am being educated by the children," Arcanus said wryly. "I suppose it's their time to get back at us."

"It is," answered Amada, "but not in the way you fear. For all these years you have given us food, shelter and clothing for our bodies. So you believe we *are* our bodies, and obviously that you are yours also. This is true; and also it is not true. Our bodies are only the vehicle for being on a planet—but who we are is individuality itself. Individuality means to be *in divine duality*, undivided paradoxical existence, undivided unity. From the outside these two pathways look like duality — body and mind, love and hate, good and bad, right and wrong and so on. And this appearance of twofoldness, di-vinity or duality, if you look at it with more or less Light, is an attribute of the third and fourth dimensions. But Who We Are resides in the juncture between the two, and that is through the tunnel of Light, which asserts our identity based in the fifth dimension and above. There only unity resides."

"Lakshmi," asked Arcanus, "are they teaching little kids philosophy in school these days?"

"Linda," he went on, turning to Amada, "I am concerned that you don't have friends and don't play enough. Do you always think such...thoughts?"

Amada replied innocently, "I do it in the presence of those whose lives lack it, and so does Haiam."

"Linda, I've told you, his name is Boy," insisted Arcanus.

"I'm sorry, my name is Amada, although you call my body Linda. Amada is truly an angelic name, as is the one my brother has," Amada said sadly, noticing the walls that Arcanus had built up. (A person's name was bestowed by the parents on Tria Ra. This was so important that females had to keep their given name until they married, and men had to keep theirs all their lives. Thus by calling myself "Haiam" rather than "Boy," I had offended the couple.)

Amada left the room.

Lakshmi looked weary. "I don't know, sweetheart," she said to her husband, "but since you've been in bed I've been having curious dreams. I see myself beautiful, on a lawn, cherishing the sun and picking flowers. My body is transparent and I feel very light and clear. Then when I wake up, I am so different from how I am in the dream that the burden of the days makes me weary and weak."

"Oh no! Now *you* are going crazy like your kids!" said Arcanus bitterly. "It looks like my stomach-hurt is making everybody else have his own fit. Well, I'm sorry to be sick! Things seem less smooth when I am sick at home. I feel like a donkey who is allowed only to work. I built this house and furnished it, I maintained it and supported you and the kids — and when I need to use my own home, everyone complains. Maybe I should go to the hospital and leave you all here!"

"Don't get me wrong," cried Lakshmi in despair, "I love you."

This was so — how else could she have lived with so little communication? This was my thought as I returned from school and read in the auric field all that had gone on.

~ ❧ ~

However, releasing all those feelings was causing my father's third, solar chakra wheel to start moving in a smoother, more balanced way. Therefore, the wheel began to generate more energy in that center. This energy created more aliveness — and therefore caused blood, nerve conduction, circulation and health to flow to the damaged organs in his belly.

The doctors had given him antacids and suppressants to help him avoid the pain. Amada and I had *given* him some pain — the kind that made him more aware of his existence.

Calling Will forward, I looked into the crystal. There I saw thousands of hospitals (the name for the buildings where the diseased lay in bed suppressing their symptoms, and where doctors were followed by drug merchants teaching them how to suppress pain). I said to Will, "I'll become a doctor, but a different kind — a healer of the Soul. Because what ultimately heals the body is the rehabilitation of the Soul's ability to come through and enliven every part of the Self."

"You got it!" said the Cat. *"The tuning of the physical instrument."*

I left my body and teleported myself into Dad's room. I spoke to him from Soul to Soul: "Beloved Master," I said, "you deserve a healthy body. You have been using it to serve. Wake up to your true mastery and go to those areas that ache. As you touch them they will be healed at once, in the physical body as well as in image, feeling and thought. This is a time for the gathering of all Masters to initially take full charge for the creation of their realities and later to transform Tria Ra in the etheric Light world that it is intended to be.

"Go and see the errors of the third wheel. All your harmful acts of the past are forgiven now, and in this forgiveness you support your Self. I love you, I support you, and I bless you. In the flesh I am your son, in the Soul I am your mirror. So forgive yourself what's past and heal it at a glance."

Arcanus' soul expanded into its etheric field and found a power line in a crystal form that radiated out into the physical, thus keeping the pain in place. The energy meld expanded into his genetic code and broke up the holding of the pain.

"William," I asked the crystal, "can you do it?"

"Yes," he replied, *"if you support me with love."*

"So be it," I said.

"So it is," echoed Arcanus. His crystal broke, and the floating pieces unleashed their energy to heal.

The Purple Rose came forth, en-Lightening the area of the body that had been blocked, and Arcanus was healed.

Coming back to my Self, I found that the operation had lasted less than a second of Tria Ra's time. "Wow!" I exclaimed.

"Yes," said the Cat, *"tuning the physical instrument is a fact. We have been discussing it since the time of earth's eviction."*

Now I recalled that on earth I had been a physician — that for a whole lifetime I had searched for ways to heal. And now I had found them.

"No action is wasted in the universe," said Augustus. *"What you don't complete in one place, you complete in another. This has to be taught so that it becomes common knowledge in peoples' lives. They think the pain is all there is, so they live in the anxiousness of now. They think it's all over, instead of realizing that life goes on and that they have a say about its movement."*

"They take life for granted," said Androgynous, *"and forget about living."*

"I see, I see what I am doing here!" And the vision arose — I was here to wake up Souls while learning to operate in a physical domain; I was here to relate to others as my Self, and to not confuse Self with body, mind or feeling. More learning to be achieved. (At this time I was not yet nine.)

"This can actually be done," I said to Will, "because all beings are healers from within."

"Yes," added L-yon, who had been witnessing this conversation in his Soul body, "but they believe doctors. And so you will be one. I have an additional name for you: Hakim Haiam. Hakim is your function—it means healer. As special as you may think it is, be humble, because the only healer that truly is, is God."

"How do you mean that?" asked Amada, who had snuck into my room in her usual silent way.

"Imagine a network," said L-yon, "and imagine each point in the network. Without the other points, there is no network. It is like a thousand points of Light. The Wholeness of the space in which the network is, is God. Therefore, can each one think of him Self as alone?"

"Certainly not!" we both replied at once.

So we grew more interested in finding out how our dad was doing. *"Well, look at him,"* said Will. We looked as the crystal magnified him. Arcanus had no pain. He was asleep in his bed, and on his face was the most peaceful smile we had ever seen on him. Around his head bluish lights whirled in pure joy.

We could enjoy our father now. And he could discover his oneness with his children.

In the other room Lakshmi, unaware of Arcanus' transformation, was crying salty, bitter tears.

Chapter 5

Initiated by Elves

Lakshmi had devoted her whole life to her husband and children, setting aside (as she now saw) her own spiritual heritage. And when she had revealed her dream of beauty to her husband, his response had made feel as if she were insane.

All through the galaxy it was the custom of the material plane to suppress awareness of all that was not matter. The energy of Being was crammed into bodies, producing behaviors that were accepted if they conformed to the rules and suppressed if they did not. These suppressive rules were called "the setting of boundaries"; distrust was so prevalent that humans believed that without those rules, everybody would behave like animals. They did.

On Tria Ra, as in the time of Pagan on earth, similar happenings were taking place. Since no one wanted to acknowledge them, no one took responsibility, so the Great Big Brother set the rules. People just turned on their programming instrument — known on earth as TV — each morning and were shown the way to live their lives.

Suppression also took place from within. People commonly said, "I'm sorry/I didn't mean that/I feel ashamed/I feel guilty" and the like. Or else they said, "Don't be silly/crazy/freaky/nutty" and so on. In all, the basic message was "Don't Be."

So humanity — a good student of this message — Was not.

And that evening Lakshmi, in her despair, wanted not to Be at all. What if I take those pills and die? she thought. I'm not happy any more, and I am tired of this game.

As she speculated on the idea, the phone rang. Lakshmi

was wanted at Grandpa's house. No children were allowed in; Amada and I had to stay next door. But we held astral hands and astroprojected into L-yon's room. Our glorious Grandpa was blessing all his sons and in-laws. He told his wife, "I am going to prepare the way. I won't leave you here too long." He closed his eyes and said his prayer: "The Lord is calling," he added. Then he closed his physical eyes and left.

The body had energies circulating through it for some time, but he was gone — so high, I couldn't even see. They buried his remains and life went on its way. His wife and daughter mourned him. Lakshmi in particular suffered from his absence.

Since L-yon and I had become good friends, he reported to me a few days later. His message was simple: "It's all true," he said. We're scared to *truly* believe that what we believe is true."

I was astonished to discover that he had been living on faith and faith alone all his life. After all, his Soul body had been communicating with me since I was small.

He had come back to prove to me and to himself that religion worked — for some. Both Amada and I had entered the material plane with knowledge of the Self. L-yon had reached this knowledge by praying all his life, and had left with knowledge of the Self. I was so happy for him and for all those who prayed. The power of prayer was transformative.

I started to pray for the maintenance of my dad's health. My prayers filled the room with thoughts that formed energy higher than matter, thus stabilizing the healing of Arcanus' Soul. Soon Dad was up and jogging.

~ ❧ ~

One morning, as my father was jogging on the street and I was sitting by a tree, I heard a tiny man speak to me. *"Hi, I'm an elf,"* he said, *"and I live in a kingdom different from yours. I understand that you have a deep interest in health — would you like to come with me?"*

Sure, I thought, why not? But how? He invited me through a door, which looked like a crack in the bark of a tree.

"Enter the crystal," Will said. And as I did, I literally projected a tiny Haiam no larger than an ant, with all the levels of Being compressed, as the diamond in its forehead illuminated the way. The elf grabbed my hand and we entered the tree.

In Tria Ra's mass consciousness only what was seen, smelled, and otherwise sensed was believable. This kept people from feeling intensely. But the joy I experienced in my new shape was tremendous!

The elf introduced himself as a friend. *"Call me Agape,"* he said. He told me he was a deva. Devas belonged to a kingdom that resembled angels, but they lived here on the ground and were interactive with the vegetal kingdom, in which they had their houses (as we did when we built homes of wood). As a deva, he had reached full integration.

"You see," he said, *"humans believe they are bodies, which prevents feeling from coming forward from the Soul. So-called enlightened ones, like yourself, believe they are a Soul – but even though you treat the body as an instrument, you still treat it as separate from the Soul. You believe you want to become a doctor, a healer; but until you know and love your Self wholly, you will have distinctions that will keep you from using your full abilities.*

"I want you to meet Herb, the king of the Devic Kingdom. He might help you understand why herbs are miracle healers."

We walked through leaves, moss and tunnels in the bark, and I saw the most exhilarating reflections of colors at this dimension. I was feeling life as never before, and I was so small that nothing could hurt me. As we walked we became smaller and smaller, until we were microscopic. The smaller my size, the better I could perceive the details of life. I recalled when I was in outer space, when the Cat expanded and shrank in size. How delightful to be this small!

My companion talked to me as we walked. Agape said, *"On this material plane humans are given an opportunity to become creators. But instead of creating the (for them) super-natural feeling of Love, they create, by their experimentation, unnatural waves. These make excessive work for us. These waves drastically altered the electromagnetic field of the earth, which affected all its matter. You think like the earth scientists – you think that light travels fast*

—but the new discoveries will show that the speed of a particle is greater than that of light. We have lived under the false impression that 'en-Lightenment' is the highest we can get. Now, on Tria Ra, chaotic wave/particles are filling the atmosphere, and we are living in a cloud of radio, TV, sonic, audio and other ELF frequencies that are too small to be seen even with the third eye. Because they cannot be seen, people think they don't exist. Thus—oh, here is Herb!"

"Continue, Agape," said the king, examining me from top to bottom.

"Thus," Agape went on, *"feelings can't be felt. So all of man's actions are for the purpose of feeling him Self."*

"Yes indeed," said Herb—a majestic little being whom I could not categorize as flower, insect or gnome. In response to my thought, he said, *"My form doesn't matter, because of the multiple mimetic characteristics I take on. I am a Soul like you, and I also am this body. Because I've raised the frequency of my body to the highest, it is one with my Soul. So my body is no longer an instrument nor is my Soul the charioteer. We are one and the same, and so is the whole vegetal kingdom."*

"So the vegetal kingdom is more evolved than the human?" I asked, full of respect and remembering what my schoolteachers had taught me.

"Evolved is not just a notion, when one is Whole. Yet it took a long time to evolve. We take care of the vegetals because they are the perfect healers for all occasions. Actually, your laboratories have taken seeds and plants and tried to mimic our effects; but they can't synthesize us. That is so in your medical world. You are a doctor, I understand."

"No," I said, "now I am only ten years old. But I want to become one." Then I caught myself—what an irony! Here I was, Haiam—beyond time and space—starting to identify with a ten-year-old boy. "I no longer know who I am," I admitted.

"That is honest," responded Herb. *"Remember: In your world arrogance prevails, and knowing and not knowing are alike.*

"I invite you to look at this: You say you want to be a healer, and this justifies the purpose of your life. Otherwise you will feel incomplete, empty. I tell you that you were born in matter once

again not to become a doctor or a healer, but to become a lover of Spirit. That is above and beyond God himself. You can come and live with us as often as you want, and learn to be a lover of your Self."

I was feeling Love — for me, for Herb, for Agape — and I loved to feel Love. There was no reward but Love itself; and as some behavior was required, I merged with Love and vowed to have it continue all the time.

"Careful," said Agape. *"It's easier to feel here. For one thing, we are smaller than the unnatural particles that are in the electric field. For another thing, we are vibrating in unison with the magnetic field of Tria Ra."*

I parted from the devas gratefully — and reluctantly.

Chapter 6

The Power of Feeling

As many times as I could, I went back to the tree where Agape was waiting for me. I kept my parallel lives going smoothly. Each time I returned to my usual shape and size, I brought back more Love for my Self. This Love penetrated all communication problems. I loved my Self so much that even Dad started to love him Self.

Lakshmi, however, still was feeling alienated. She was now such a sensitive Being that I rarely understood her. One day I asked Herb about her.

"Your beautiful mother loves to feel," he said, *"like all people do there. The problem is that they want to feel joy and love and life, but their emotions are so blocked that they use the emotional energy to create drama for themselves. Through this drama they can feel — and so their Soul feels itself, having created the drama. This drama is the result of their conditioning.*

"People get hurt and beaten down that way, but the mass consciousness keeps them from seeing that they *have created it. Then they hurt their fellow man."*

"What can I do for her?" I asked earnestly. "She is my mother in the flesh. And maybe in the Soul."

"Who cares?" asked Herb. *"If you want to do for her, do more for your Self."*

"What's that?"

"You always want to 'heal' and 'serve' and 'do.' Don't you know that you came here to pass your test for you? *You created all of this to feel. You Were, you Are, you Will Be! You know Oneness, Beauty, Glory, Wisdom and the like. But Tria Ra is not earth, not the stars, not the All — it's where you have to feel.* ***You created***

your etheric, and therein, by will, your thought. The thought moved and felt an image, and you're in a body, complete. All that's missing is your memory that you created all."

"I know, I know, I know," now feeling irritated and dumb.

"Great, you are feeling **something.** *The more you feel your feelings, the more you'll feel your body – and when this Whole that you are fills the body wholly, you will be like us, an integrated Being. Each part of the body will become alive."*

"And," mocked Agape and Herb together, *"you know, you know, you know."*

"You know you did it," said Herb more gently. *"But do you know why?"*

Augustus was mute; Androgynous looked away; Beauty smiled; Forgiveness bowed; the Cat reached out at a fly. *"No,"* they told me, *don't look for help. Not even God will help you now. You, creator, created all of this for a reason. The same reason peace happened;* ***the same reason the Council of Twelve dissolved; the same reason –***

"To **feel** yourself, oh Lord. You can only see in others what exists in you. You can feel in others only that which is in you."

And Herb sang:

Flowers, breezes, roses, freezes,
heat waves, crushes, fights, and loves
all together is arranged,
as a mirror to be loved.

It is Self in adoration,
in the feeling of creation,
in the sexual mate of Self,
in the Wholeness of the elf.

Now's the time to integrate
What in hours you'd create;
now's the moment to be born,
releasing passion from a thorn.

Soon thirteen years of age,
You'll have new emotions, love and rage,
but if you can feel your Whole
you will truly be a Soul.

As Soul in body
can empower
day by day
and every hour,
the healing forces from within
no longer will be just a whim;
the dark influences from without
no longer will have might.

And as he finished, I knew that the powers of herbs had been released and that the world would never again be the same.

Chapter 7

Puma

"Why are you so excited?" asked Mom as I walked into the garden.

"It's springtime," Dad answered for me, "and tomorrow Boy will be a teenager. It's time he gets initiated into life." Arcanus had left his city job, and now spent his days enjoying himself in our vegetable garden, which, because of his knowledge of finances, had become not only a delightful pastime but also a magnificent business. "In the old days," he went on, "youngsters were taken to the jungle and taught to hunt. Then they took a wife, and from then on had their own life."

"And what," asked Amada, "were girls supposed to do at thirteen?" Even though she was only twelve, she looked like fifteen. All the boys on the block wanted to be my friend just so I would let them into Amada's house. An adorable young girl who already had her monthly period, she was considered a woman.

Only Lakshmi was not doing well. She was still having fears about being crazy. This was because she withheld the openness of her consciousness from herself. Amada and I were clearly aware of this, but we would not invade her inner dialogue unless she invited us in. We knew the time would come when she would open up; hopefully, she could balance both worlds. Lakshmi wrote in her journal, "I feel terrible. I see the presence of my father all the time, but I can't hear him. It seems he is trying to give me a message of some kind — but I know he is dead. How can this be? It must be because I didn't love him enough. Now I feel guilty, like my brain is exploding."

For me, since my encounter with Agape, Herb and the devas, these two worlds were becoming truly one. I spent many hours walking in the woods, enjoying the smell of pines and eucalyptus trees and delighting in my own creation. The silence of the woods opened my heart even more to the completion of Creation, and I started to take note of my feelings in order to record what I liked to do. Becoming a healer was now secondary to loving. I didn't ask too many questions; I just enjoyed my Self.

In the meantime, Tria Ra was approaching a big war among its people — much like the war on earth, but with electronic weapons. The intention was to control mass consciousness by altering the wavelength of the auric fields. The power of Imago, lord of the astral realm — a discarnate entity who never learned to feel love on earth — had reached Tria Ra. As I approached full puberty, I started to be concerned.

~ ❧ ~

Journeying through the woods in my natural shape and form, I started to relate to animals as well as vegetals. They were an interesting type of life — the experience of feelings was always in the air. The deeper I went in the woods, the more I found myself at the edge of danger. Sometimes I went camping by myself, sometimes with school companions. But I always had the same adventure — the more I experienced danger and fear about the survival of my body, the more excitement I felt.

One night my friends Joe Teen, Jim Kid and I were sitting next to a tree when our fire went out. In that dark night (no moon, no stars, just clouds), two lanternlike, catty eyes appeared only a few feet away. We all saw them at once, and we froze. My heart pumping, my skin wet with perspiration, I stared at this sensible big beast — and in one leap jumped up onto a branch, followed immediately by my two companions. Had they hesitated for only a few seconds, their bodies would have been badly scratched.

We spent the whole night in the tree, scared and utterly excited. The puma waited patiently, giving each leaf that fell from our tree his full attention. I realized that this big beast could have eaten us all — and, in the feeling of the moment, my whole body vibrated. I was fully there in each cell, even in my balls (a part of the body that usually is considered a forbidden zone). It was as if I were a tiger or a leopard — there was no thought, just total concentration.

As the sun rose, the puma's mate came by. Together they roared and scratched and played. Suddenly, Joe moved slightly on his branch; the pumas stopped their game and watched us, fully aware of our presence. At last they turned from us and mated.

The spectacle was dramatically, shockingly, beautifully awesome. My lower wheels started churning as my own sexuality came awake in the presence of these animals — these totally uninhibited, unveiled, forceful, completely aggressive yet loving beasts.

As I watched them (focusing on protecting my Self), a sense of ecstasy invaded by own being.

The Cat came present in my field. *"Remember me,"* he said. *"Now do you know why I came to you as strength, in this form?*

"The lower centers awaken when you are really in the body. This is a vital step for integration; watch the animals' movements. See for yourself that all you see, feel and like or dislike in others, you create your Self — as a reflection of your feelings so that you can express them. Do not suppress — or, if you must suppress, suppress suppression!"

I felt as if the area from my belly to my groin had independent life. It pulsated, beat and danced to its own rhythm. I knew I was immortal.

But how long would I have to sit in the tree?

"Become the cat," said the Cat.

I was perplexed. But from the deeps of my guts, I roared. I roared so loud that Jim and Joe were shocked and scared, thinking I had become some kind of "cat man." My roar was so profound that it could have come from a hundred lions. The pumas ran away in fear.

Maybe this was the initiation my father had mentioned — the battle of the beast. I started laughing as Jim and Joe and I climbed down the tree. They were still staring at me in horror. To calm them I started joking, saying that I had seen Tarzan roar like that. But my roar had been too authentic. My friends were now my ex-friends. But they also were no longer kids or teens. There was no way to cover this one up.

~ ❧ ~

"Where have you been?" asked Amada when I returned. "You look like a wild beast!"

I had always seen her as adorable, but now for the first time I saw her more as a voluptuous woman than as her etheric self. "I *am* a beast," I announced, "and soon I'll have my woman! Remember what Dad said."

Instantly Amada perceived my night's adventure. The murmur that was awakened in my body reached her and she too began to pulsate. "I feel it also," she said. "Now we have lost our innocent purity. We feel our gender, and people here say that it is bad."

"Amada," I said, "How can it be bad if it is what all Creation feels and does? That's the drawback of religion—it tries to say what's good or bad."

"Doesn't such a feeling suppress the expression of the Soul?" she asked.

I showed her my genitals and asked her to feel them. Clearly she enjoyed it, yet was shy. I wondered whether all brothers and sisters didn't play with each other's feelings.

Augustus whispered in my ear, *"Be wise—let her find this out outside the inner circle of home. You, my friend, will get your chance soon."*

~ ❧ ~

I was obsessed with the vision of mating. I recalled the energy of the pumas—such a perfect dance, such perfect balance, so complete. I saw the act of mating in all the creation process. Everything and everybody was mating with each other. To suppress mating was to suppress the God-given Oneness. It was duality that was the source of this suppression, that enabled machine-regulated programs to rule the worlds.

It made sense that the Council of Twelve had dissolved the

apparent quiet harmony throughout the galaxy to bring forth the electrical manifestation of friction through emotion. God could thereby feel Himself in every act, becoming an active participant rather than a mere observer and consciously aware of His creation.

As I played with my genitals, the sperm — the seeds of life — were there. I looked at my first ejaculation, and with my wholesome Self I perceived the miracle of Life in the presence of these seeds.

Definitely, no sin was here! And as the Creator did not judge creative reproduction as sinful, I did not understand how humans had judged it so. Because Imago was a disembodied entity, he lacked the possibility of the sexual act. So he implanted the idea that bodies were degraded into the imagination of man, thereby taking his revenge. And humans, not understanding this, considered their bodies as perverse, sinful entities.

Was this the only reason to be alive in a body? Now I could understand what I never understood on earth: Love — the outermost flow of feeling — had a right to fully Be and to fully express itself throughout all the ways of Self.

At this time, when I saw clearly why feeling was so important, I had not yet turned fourteen.

Chapter 8

The Light

I was vacationing at a beautiful beach with my family, participating actively in this normal, everyday life, dancing with girls yet never losing the perspective of the divineness of my Self. Each time I remembered the mating of the pumas, I experienced desire. While this passion was not lustful, it was completely present in the body and thus it vitalized all my actions.

One day as I was diving deep in the sea, a dolphin came and started to swim around. Up to now I had seen dolphins only in photographs, so the real-life beauty of this mammal amazed me. The dolphin vibrated an electromagnetic spectrum that was instantly translated into language as soon as it reached my brain. What he said was, *"Your passion will be quenched if you learn to use it well. You think it's just for woman. It is, in part – but truly it's for God."*

"Passion?" I asked in surprise. "What does that have to do with God?"

"Passion is a fuel for creativity," the dolphin replied. *"Your sperm contains the God force – for pleasure, new life; and each time it is released, the Light comes out, seeking understanding. Each sperm is a possibility of Self and Life. Now, in your youth, you use it for fun, but later you will realize that its purpose is to create your son."*

"My son!" I said in amazement. "I can't have a son – I'm just a teenager."

"Yes, you can – but you won't yet. You humans have learned to have children according to the world's timing, not nature's, just as you eat according to the clock and do not rest according to the

stars. You here on Tria Ra once again have forgotten the nature of real living; and for this you'll be wiped away."

"Oh God," I said, experiencing so many of the feelings I'd had on earth. "Not another holocaust! How can it be prevented?"

"By loving your Selves more than you love all else," the dolphin replied.

"But how can that be achieved for all?"

"You don't need ***all****. If only one out of ten does it, the vibration of Love around him engulfs the other nine. No matter what they feel, these feelings will be neutralized. It is like erecting radio transmitters in different spots on Tria Ra or like doing acupuncture on different points of the planet. A network can be established through which people help each other by sending out thoughts of white Light, Love, and friendly energies to counteract the vibrations produced by the bad news inflicted by the press and other forces upon the mind of man.*

"The opening of the heart neutralizes the dark force of negativity." Then he said, *"Your passion will be satisfied. Come to the beach tonight."*

And from the depths of the ocean, an imageless Light of Love sprang forward, creating a ripple that parted the bottom of the ocean. I swam up with this Light onto the shores of Tria Ra.

"I am the force of Positivity," it said. *"I battle Imago, for now you need to know that I am willing to awaken the neutralizing elements in your planet to counteract the forces of possession that false imagination has inflicted on people.*

"I have news for you. The astral plane, which everyone considers real, is just a creation of humanity's unfulfilled desires. Therefore, my force can dissolve Imago as well as all the astral entities that try to dominate this world and worlds to come. Earth was like this; but even Pagan and his like could have changed had they been challenged by my Love.

"I am that which empowers all Beings throughout their lives, and all in their lives is creativity – they are always creating, even when they don't know it. So in their last movement, I am still with them.

"Many have believed that I am God, but I am but a humble servant of the Lord. I am what has been called the Spirit's force.

"When the Soul thinks of a creation, that thought moves to the feeling plane and the body acts. I intervene in the intermediate step from feeling to visualization, erasing the blockages and allowing the manifestation to come into Being.

"But I have to be called upon, and that's the difference between me and Imago. He comes and takes control; I come when I am called. I could help people convert all nuclear plants into museums, all warheads into playgrounds, if the world could just conceive it that way."

"Positive thinking?" I asked this Force.

"Not exactly," it replied. *"More like a vehicle for true affirmation of life."*

In this presence there was no more image than in the whirling of Love and Light around itself. I watched it in fascination.

I also noticed a beautiful woman off to the side, sitting on sand. She was around my age, tall and tanned, with long, straight black hair and a beautiful body that moved subtly but invitingly.

"You would like to be with her?" asked the Force, interrupting my thoughts.

"Wow," I said, "it looks like anything I think or say to myself is public, except for my fellow humans."

"The whole universe is always listening," it replied. *"People are the only ones who don't realize it. Whatever you ask is always given. If the manifestation takes time, this is because people rarely ask directly — their requests are filtered through other things they're wanting. People pray for something, but they are under Imago's influence; so instead of making a prayer that goes to the Essence of what they want, they wrap it up in all the other things they've asked for. So they get all the other stuff first.*

"Then their feelings bounce back from all that they now feel they didn't ask for, and these feelings become aggressors against the Self. These are called negative emotions. Anger, fear, sadness, frustration, which people commonly experience, are reflected emo-

tions, bouncing back the images that are between our intended goals and the obstacles in the way. Have you noticed that we never get angry or sad at people or situations that we don't care about? Energy, when set in motion and stopped by the false images, doesn't reach its destiny; thus we experience these reflected emotions.

"If the actions they take are unaligned with their original intention, anger shows up, and if they persist, this anger blocks their Soul in sadness. When this action persists, the blockage becomes so thick that they fear for their survival.

"When they get stuck in this fear – which can sometimes (as you may remember) happen in the birth canal – they live their lives wearing masks in order to have an identity, or they spend their life praying for decorations of their mask in order to feel them Selves. Thus they create unnecessary events in order to feel their Soul. But they don't get to feel their Souls; what most people feel are the blockages in their bodies from their past disappointments and the fear that their expectations won't be met.

"So if you call upon me, I can help you neutralize these images – not only in yourself, but also in others – and thus get what you truly desire."

"Are you an astral entity?"

"No," said the Force, *"but I am useful there."*

"Are you a feeling? Yes, you must be, since I feel the Love."

"No," said the Force, *"but I am useful there also."*

"You definitely are not physical, I know, but you could be very useful here!"

"Exactly," it responded.

"So who are you?"

"Do you really want to know?"

I centered. I really did not care. There was no thought, no form, no image of my Self. I called forth the qualities of Essence, but even they were not interested in finding out. Relaxing deeply, I walked into this whirl of Life.

> Inside it, I heard the sound of Heart.
> The sound of Heart,
> which calls within,
> just says *"Come home.*

I who am,
who truly am,
I wait in love
in everlasting love
for everlasting times
for you, true love.

"Through your senses
who I am leaves
and goes
and goes and goes
to mind, to things,
to space, to time,
to man and woman
old or young.
But since I am
Eternal Source
I wait and know
one day you'll come
back inside to me
and stay with one another.

"Curious drive
which flees to live,
which searches out
and out
and out –
how could you ever find
the word which is inside?

"The word of God,
the Love within –
for so long
I spoke
and felt
and thought –
and now
I do not dare to say
'I know what is,'
but I sense I've found.

"I can see what is within
and what outside
could all be one.
And yet when mind is gross
and coarse,
when heart is subtle and pure,
there and only there
am I satisfied.

"Allah or God,
the source of peace
the Christ within
the word of Love
the Enlightened One
was called –
and all I feel
is calm and clear.

"There is a power in this grace.
The truth is all in sight.
I am knocking at the door behind the heart.
No prayer, meditative thought or wine
Intoxicates me like this one.

"For so long we wander
all around
and at the turn of time
it finds you
and says you're mine,
the true and perfect one,
coming home again after endless roads
to where it all began –
in Love."

As I stepped out of this whirling I was transformed. My passion was quenched for now; instead of its being a bodily reaction — instead of it generating me — I could now generate *it*.

I had become resourceful about my gender, and I noticed a difference (which progressively showed itself over later years) — that I had no need to demonstrate my manhood competitively (competitiveness being the way of the world). Thus competitiveness was replaced by competence, and this competence allowed me to perform with optimum results.

The Light was always with me, yet I would learn to relate to it for my demands, always calling it in with a little prayer: "May this happen in the Light for the highest Good of All." It was a fantastic tool for achievement, without the compulsion to achieve, and the more I trusted what took place, the more content I was. How different from what was taught in school! There, achievement always looked separated from, and external to, the Self. Acceptance was molded into resignation, surrender became submission, and the power of inquiry was called curiosity and considered frivolous (if considered at all).

~ ❧ ~

The night of my encounter with the Light I found myself on the beach, according to the dolphin's instructions.

Each evening at the yacht club there was a dance for high school kids. I danced enjoyably for awhile, and then sat down to rest. At my table was the girl I had noticed earlier on the beach. She smiled at me, and my whole body shook.

"Hi," I said shyly, feeling exposed, as if she knew my thoughts.

"Hello," she replied in a friendly way.

"What's your name?"

"Bhakti-Shadai," she responded.

"'Bhakti-Shadai' — like this beautiful night! And you are such a beautiful girl."

She laughed with shyness and pleasure. I looked into her eyes, as if to apologize for my own shyness. She was not just a beautiful girl — she was a radiant light and a sensuous woman. I felt already in love, and I censored myself for going so fast. Calling in the Light, I prayed, "Let be what is for the highest good."

"Okay," responded the Light, and thus I was relieved from my own pressure to feel close.

While my prayer was going on silently, she was laughing —

which embarrassed me even more. "Like to dance?" I asked, to interrupt the too-quick intimacy.

"Sure, why not," she agreed.

Movement would relieve the stress, I thought, noticing that my whole body vibrated with the same passion I had felt before when alone, but now was directed toward her.

"This is your Soulmate," said Augustus, *"so relax, no need to rush. Luckily, you found her early in your life, so you'll be able to recognize the quality of what a Soulmate is."*

"Go dance," added the Cat. *"This night is full of fun!"*

Chapter 9

Bhakti-Shadai

We moved as if we were two halves of one whole for hours and hours. Finally exhausted, we decided to walk on the beach. Our bodies were wet with perspiration, and our Selves were completely attuned to the rhythms that came primordially from within and that resonated with the music of the records.

"What a wonderful night!" said Bhakti-Shadai. "Look at the lights in the sky, the shadows on the moon—and look at that!" A shooting star fell.

I touched her hand, and a feeling of ecstasy shot through my whole body.

"Exquisite night," she whispered. The ocean breeze caressed our bodies as we walked on the warm sand. It was such a liberating feeling to be alive. I was so full of my Self that I wished those moments were eternal.

Never in my whole life had I felt so much so quickly, so deeply, so empathetically for another human being. It was passion in the fullest sense of the word—not in its lustful representation, but in the fullness of Life expressing its Self in maximum resonance with another Self who felt like my own.

I experienced a wonderful feeling in my loins, which were so filled with throbbing energy that I felt as if I would burst. I stopped and looked into Bhakti-Shadai's honey-brown eyes, and there I saw my Self. "I love you," I said shyly but deeply. This was the strongest statement I had ever made.

"You do?" she asked flirtatiously. And she started to move away, embarrassed by my declaration.

I held onto her hand. "Yes, I loved you the first moment I saw you. I feel we are meant to be together. I feel so much for you," and tears rolled from my eyes. This made incarnation worthwhile! It made all my discoveries and pains throughout my lifetimes worthwhile. It was as if I had found my Self.

She smiled warmly. "I know what you mean. I feel the same; but you, being a man, must be used to this. For me, it's the first time."

This statement expanded my joy even more. I didn't know how to tell her that I knew we were Soulmates, that we were One and the same, and that no matter how many men or women through the ages had been with us, this was it — completion at last.

"Look at our romantic Haiam," said the Cat teasingly. *"We didn't know that we had to come to Tria Ra to find out you were a romantic."*

"Shh," I silenced the Cat for the first time in our lifelong interaction. "Shut up."

"Don't say that," said Augustus. *"He is your strength. You don't want to shut it off just because you are in love."*

Infatuation is dangerous, I thought; maybe I should withhold. At that moment her tender, voluptuous lips touched mine softly, igniting me with fire and scattering my thoughts to nowhere.

"Sensational!" I said. "Your touch is sensational! I need you, I want you, I love you!"

She laughed, and I would recall her laughter through eternity. Its ripples penetrated my etheric field as we rolled together on the ground in a unifying embrace. We rubbed against each other in a rapture of love, which incited us to play, caress and kiss all over our bodies — ecstatically, completely feeling the joy of each other's presence. But as we were about to make love, we were surrounded by a purple Light. It felt warm and seemed to resonate with our Souls. It came from above, slightly to the side, and a stairway seemed to come down from the center of it. A high-pitched note invited us to ascend; and even though it crossed our minds to run away, we held hands and started walking up. At each step the sound was more acute; and just as this note engulfed us, we stepped into a silver metallic ship stationed in the sky.

"Bhakti-Shadai and Hakim," a voice said, *"welcome to Mercab."*

I knew that voice—it was the same voice that had welcomed me to the All when the GFH had exploded; the same voice that had told me about earth's true history and about the attributes of Essence I would be meeting.

"Hakim," repeated Bhakti-Shadai. "Isn't your name Haiam?"

"Yes, both," I whispered. "Don't be afraid. These are my friends."

"If you're one of them, now I'm even more afraid."

"No, I'm not—or at least not more than you are. And I promise this is the first encounter of this kind," I said (thinking, at least in a long time).

So I said to the voice, "Thanks in the name of both of us for your invitation."

"You are welcome. Mercab invites you both to come with us for a journey to Source. Since you are both One, you have earned your right to travel. You will be shown how to use your passion."

"What do they know about us?" whispered Bhakti-Shadai apprehensively. "How long were they watching us on the beach? I hope they don't tell on us. Mother would be shocked. I am just a girl." She was stuttering, and tears were rolling from her eyes.

This made me love her even more. I felt so strong, caring and protective of her. I felt so whole, such a man. At the same time, I didn't want to impose on her and tell all I felt I knew about us. Bhakti-Shadai was worried that if we took this trip, she would get home too late; yet I knew that if we went to Source, there would be no travel time—the theory of relativity had long been superseded by speeds that were ten times higher than the speed of light.

"Wondrous humans," said the voice, *"if you are willing to travel, you will be back in what is called one hour before we encountered you—actually, before you finished dancing at the club. But you don't have to come if you choose not to. This is a gift*

and a privilege to be bestowed. It also is honoring the promise of the dolphin."

"What?" Bhakti-Shadai asked. "What dolphin?"

"Flipper," I joked.

She smiled nervously, then released the tension with a laugh. "All right," she said impulsively. "But promise that we will be back an hour earlier than when we left!" She could make this light-hearted remark because of her instantaneous openness to accept what was outside her order of thought.

Zoom! And we were there.

Chapter 10

Visit to Mercab

Mercab was the remnant of what the Council of Twelve had once used as the seat of the Galactic Alliance.

It still existed in the material plane, but at a level of evolution in another dimensionality. In this dimension bodies had refined them Selves. They looked golden and transparent; no negativity entered the magnetic fields of Source.

These Beings did not reproduce them Selves. There was no need for reproduction, since nobody ever died or was diseased. They lived harmoniously, preserving the infrastructure of the place, making it ready for the complete evolution of Beings who individually would discover their sameness with the Lord, yet the uniqueness of their ways. Then and only then would Mercab — the support mechanism — disappear, dematerializing itself and allowing the Council of Twelve to rule again, this time duplicating Source in the Wholeness of each individual Being.

"In order for this to happen," the voice told us, *"we have chosen your children as the Adam and Eve of a new race. Your son will be the bliss of the Elohim, and his name will be Eliyanand. Your daughter is foreverness; her name will be Aeterna."*

"Our children!" we exclaimed simultaneously.

"Yes, each in their own right as male and female will originate the Wholeness of the Twelve in One."

"But we don't have children!" we continued in one voice.

"You do and you don't," responded the voice. And a holographic picture of the children was projected onto a huge screen. Recognizing our Selves in it, we cried and laughed and danced.

(These children, my dear ones, are you!)

"But this will happen later, when you are prepared. We brought you here to give you blessings and show you your purpose — why you are on Tria Ra."

"I thought my purpose," said Bhakti-Shadai, "was to be a dancer."

"And mine to be a healer and to love my Self," I said.

"Too many years of dogmas," answered the voice, *"have made you believe that there is only one purpose. Indeed, the purpose is to Be; but that can take as many forms, types and functions as there are people."*

"Most people don't understand unity in multiplicity too well," I said arrogantly.

"Exactly — and you understand it less than all," responded the voice. *"Just because you were clear didn't mean you didn't need a body. You still needed a body in order to learn to feel. We will let you know when the last lesson comes. It hasn't yet."*

"What should we do together?" I asked.

"Keep on breathing," the voice answered, as Bhakti-Shadai embraced me lovingly.

"I think I understand," I said, turning to my beloved. "Long ago we were making love on a beach on earth — "

"Yes!" she interrupted excitedly, "that's when I was Agna!"

"Yes, and at that time we had the passion but didn't know where to go with it. Then I got married to someone else, the earth blew up, and I never saw you again."

"Never until today," she answered triumphantly.

The visit to Mercab was coming to a close. We were teleported smoothly back to the spaceship. In the snap of an eye we were back on Tria Ra walking out from the yachting club after the dance.

"Wow!" blinked Bhakti-Shadai, "I just had a daydream!"

"So did I," I responded. But the closeness that we felt in the familiarity of our new relationship told us that it had been no daydream.

We'd been home.

Chapter 11

Lakshmi Opens Up

During the next few years I witnessed myself growing up.

My relationship with Bhakti-Shadai was always full of love, yet we had never brought it to a sexual manifestation. We were companions, supporting each other's needs and learning to project toward the future a vision that at this time was not totally clear.

My father and I had become more open and communicative about daily matters, each enjoying this mutual receptivity, yet avoiding the dynamics of our inner lives. After his ulcer had healed, he became very serious about taking care of himself. He pursued various activities to relax himself, using most of his time to work in his garden. This work nourished him.

Lakshmi had experienced her own ailments. She had withdrawn from the outside world and directed her energies toward her inner life. She had finally accepted the inner communication from her father, and L-yon reported to me that he was teaching her from the other side what she had been unable to accept while he was alive.

One day out of my own need to communicate with her, I decided to break our isolation. My grandfather had authorized me to disclose our secret.

"Mom, do you know I speak with Grandpa?" I asked her tentatively.

"Don't make fun of me," she snapped, seeming hurt. "That's nonsense and you know it."

This was how human beings, both on earth and Tria Ra, were suppressed — there was no permission to express what was going on, because such notions were judged "nonsensical," "silly" or "insane," according to the intensity of the experience. Thus mental hospitals were filled with people whose relatives and acquaintances panicked when they made such statements. Fearing the abnormal (just as I did in outer space, when I refused at first to accept the Cat's changing sizes), these friends and relatives refused to accept any "abnormal" communications, which usually intimidated the person into withdrawing and denying the experience for fear of being discovered. Few dared to express what they felt.

In the same way, creativity and new ways of perceiving were stifled by the rigid norms of association. Creativity — the act of creating, or bringing forward from nothing — had been replaced with a process of association, in which objects or situations encountered in one context were recombined by association and then presented in a different context. Obviously there was no Sourceful originality, since the computer could do this kind of recombination more efficiently.

But colleges and institutions of higher learning gave diplomas to students who became experts in all fields just by reading about subjects, rather than by using their power of creation. Thus early in their lives they were considered authorities by others who therefore no longer dared to express. The more books these experts read, the more they thought they knew. Wisdom was replaced by information, education by indoctrination, and creative thinking by the chattering mind.

Most people's minds manifested in fragmented communication, since spontaneous sharing was obsolete, being judged impulsive. Intuitive knowing was viewed as a phenomenon to be studied and researched, and those who did it tried to measure it with tools that measured the effects, not the source. Thus the arrogance of limitation prevailed.

So it was in the midst of this culture — which did not care about the quality of living, the greatness of the Soul or the Wholeness of humanity — that Lakshmi lived, embarrassed about her natural abilities, which had knocked at her inner door from time immemorial to be expressed.

Her sensitivity was so extreme and her kindness so refined

that even had she not been my loving mother, I would have wanted to connect with this Being for the sake of Life itself.

"Mother," I asserted, "remember that you are my mother and that I love you very, very much."

"Yes," she said, "I know, but you like to make fun of me. You both do, you and your sister, when you say those things. Years ago Linda was so insistent on talking about these things. But I never wanted to — it is private."

"Private," I responded, observing therefore that something existed. "You mean you don't *want* to share it."

I hadn't known that Amada had ever insisted on the subject. I had seen little of her in the last few years, since she had taken a boyfriend and was rarely home. Alas, I thought, she should have told me. I wouldn't have withheld my Self from Lakshmi so long.

I was crying in remorse at not having helped my mother to open up earlier, when L-yon's presence came in and spoke to me discreetly: *"There is a right time and place for each circumstance."*

All right, I nodded to my Self.

"Who are you talking to?" my mother asked.

A spaceman, I wanted to say, but her mood was not ready for jokes. So I said, "Mother, we have to talk very seriously about this. First of all, you need to know that I never thought you were crazy. I never judged you for any of this; on the contrary, I rejoiced when you first began to dream of another world."

Hearing my voice so calm and assured, she started to listen with care.

"I myself," I added, "have been communicating with Beings outside the material plane throughout all my life. I even see them sometimes, and they are as clear and real as you are. I have learned not to say much about it but to listen to what they try to teach. I have become..." (I wanted to say "a better human being," since that was usually the term that might most convince humans to open up, but instead I went for authenticity) "...an integrated Soul who is learning to live in the material plane, without sacrificing the knowledge of I Am."

"You must have been speaking to L-yon!" she said enthusiastically. "What you are saying sounds like what he has been telling me for years."

"Yes, years while he was in his body — because he was your father and knew Who You Were before you even came into his household. And the same happened with me. The difference was, as I recall, that at my first birthday party, while everyone was celebrating my body's age, he and I dialogued in the eternity of our Souls."

"Do you mean you believe you really have a Soul?" asked Lakshmi, the same whose Soul I fell in love with from outer space. But such were the conditions of mental suppression in the material plane that even something as true as the Soul was seen only as a tentative possibility here.

"No," I said, shocking her, "I don't believe I *have* a Soul."

"Good," she said, falling rapidly for my trick, "I was getting concerned that you too would need a shrink."

"I *am* a Soul," I continued, "and what I think we all need is an expander, since living in this little box is depressing and oppressing Who We Are."

"I am hesitant to believe this," she said, beginning to weep. "And yet I want to believe it, I want it to be true. For years I've been speaking with presences that are not physical, so I could never relate to them fully. If I did, it was hard to speak about it with the family or risk losing all my friends. How could I have shared the ambiguity about realities with others?"

I thought into my crystal and requested Grandpa to come. He perceived that I wanted to see him for this occasion, and as the diamond in my forehead filled the room with Light, L-yon teleported and materialized. He physically appeared, looking as he had weeks before he died so that we could all remember him as he had been. *"Dear daughter,"* he said, *"why didn't you ever ask me to come this way?"*

"I never thought of it," she sobbed. "Daddy, Daddy, I missed you so much. From my early childhood I was angry at you because you were so absorbed in your religion and didn't pay attention to me. I needed your love, and when you died I realized how much I cared for you. So I started thinking of you, and you came to me; but I interpreted that as just missing you. Naturally, the doctors thought I was hallucinating, and it scared me."

Now I saw mother's emotional Self, which had been arrested at a very early age in her physical development, come alive. Her judgment of her father had covered her Soul with resentment both for herself and for him. Therefore she could not express true Love. This kind of suppression happened with many people on Tria Ra.

Later she dedicated her whole life to recovering the lost connection, and in order to do that she pleased her father, her husband, her friends. She became known as a pleaser. The stability of the underlying Essence had enabled her to be committed — but pleasing was what she was committed to. The lack of authenticity had caused a reversal of the energy, thus causing many ailments. Now, having compassionately recognized her need for love and receiving it, she was instantly healed and freed from all ailments. Her feeling capacity was restored.

For hours she sat and was held in her father's lap. Her emotional Being grew up — maturing, rejoining, and starting to accept the Beauty of her Soul. She was freed from negativity when the crystallized judgment of her early childhood about her father and her Self cracked open. And as this thought form was released, her feelings came alive.

"Healing can happen in an instant," said Augustus. *"It need not take years of analysis."*

And as her emotional Self was growing up into her chronological age, she integrated her mind with the Oneness of her Soul; because her intellect — and then her whole environment — needed to be reeducated.

So I called forth the Light of Love for the highest good, and a purple flame burned away the negativity, transmuting and dissolving all pain and sorrow, allowing her to discover her own qualities of Essence.

L-yon's teaching — his role as a father — was not complete. Lakshmi and L-yon looked at each other as equals and forgave each other for all misunderstandings. Because there was no longer any judgment, Lakshmi had become her Self again.

"Mother," said Amada, entering the room and totally ignoring L-yon, "you look so *good.* I've been waiting eighteen years to speak with you! Do you know that you and I lived together many times?" And she went into an extensive explanation about the Atlantean civilization, where she remembered Lakshmi and herself as sisters.

"That's nice," I said, "but what are we going to do with Dad?" At the precise moment when I had that thought, the door opened and Arcanus walked in smiling. When he saw L-yon, his eyes crossed and he collapsed like a bag of potatoes on the floor.

"Too much is too much," said L-yon, dematerializing.

Chapter 12

Medical School

This experience of unity in the family was a turning point.

The stress of seeing L-yon proved too much for Arcanus. His ulcer reactivated, which impaired his mood once again. But this time he was more open than he had been the last time he got sick. The discovery of Soul unity among Lakshmi, Amada and me had stabilized our friendship, enabling us to operate as a team. Our household experienced none of the typical conflicts of adolescence (lack-of-Essence) to which all my classmates had fallen prey. Now that my mother had (cautiously) opened, Soul communication was the order of the day.

Since Arcanus constantly resisted our explanations, all we could do for him was to love him, finally realizing that he had created this event in order to begin communication with the Soul.

A long time went by. We were patient, understanding that he needed time to overcome his limitations.

My friendship with Bhakti-Shadai had moved into different dimensions. I was occupied with my college activities and left myself little time for play. These years went by in a kind of haze. There were opportunities to be part of the team and engage in group activities. It was a good occasion to indulge in mass consciousness — enough to find out Imago's ability to control.

Augustus recorded the experience in my Soul, the trials and errors as well as obstructions. I seemed to learn the nature of this world: I engaged in temporary sexual affairs, yet I always kept my energy for the day when Bhakti-Shadai and I would merge. But since I lived at school, a distance from home, I hardly ever saw her.

The year I began medical school, I proposed marriage. "Bhakti-Shadai," I said, "it's time to get serious. Let us start a home." But she asked for a raincheck on this offer, even though we were in love with each other. So I assumed she wanted to experience her Self some more. I felt hurt and rejected, but in the depth of my Being I had so much certainty and hope for us that this refusal seemed to leave no mark.

Learning medicine was an interesting endeavor. I had embarked on a lifetime commitment to healing, so I knew that medical school was only an introduction to *one* of the ways of healing. Although the true path of healing was the path of the warrior, in which each of our wounds needs to be integrated, Tria Ra's medical schools were concerned only with mechanics. They saw the human as a body that had a mind, even though (as I argued) this was only a belief. So ninety-nine percent of the warriors were destined to dissect corpses kept in freezers and look at test tubes, microscopes and lab work in which no living entity was present. Each time I inquired about the purpose of it all, I was told I'd never be a doctor if I kept asking philosophical questions.

We studied day and night. There was so much information to devour. Books and more books, thousands of dead papers, experiments that had no connection with health.

One teacher told me that in order to understand the healthy body, we had to know the sick body. Whatever wasn't sick might, by exclusion, be considered healthy.

During this time, William was my best friend. I learned to appreciate him and the discipline of sitting for hours and hours concentrating on books, which, as I incorporated their contents, started to make sense.

"Amada," I said one day while visiting at home, "this is so hard! I already know, just as you do, how the physical instrument becomes timid. How did I get myself into this school of information? Do you know that my classmates are having nervous breakdowns right and left? They can't resist the stress."

Universities, evidently, were stress machines. Young athletic people were suffering from what was labeled anxiety, depression, ulcers, heart attacks, interpersonal conflicts, violence, drug abuse and similar man-produced ailments. Thousands of students were dropping out of careers less coveted than medicine because there were no prospective jobs for them upon graduation. Computer operators were produced in large numbers for a market that absorbed them voraciously.

It was the age of information. Everyone had to know everything. The negative emotions thus produced created a blockage around the third wheel of the human instrument, at the solar plexus (the seat of reactivity); and the magnetic force's friend, Imago, did a great job in the development of the alter ego.

"What's the alter ego?" asked Amada.

"It's false identity," I replied. "It reduces the flow of energy to the lower half of the body and your entire energy field — the brain operates only to regulate the false."

"That's why everybody is saying 'be *somebody*,'" she agreed. "No one is saying 'just Be.'"

And she started to sing this song:

> Freedom is surrender
> and this surrender is Love.
> Love that always Was
> Love that always Is
> Love that will always Be.
> True Love is to remember
> that which I truly Am
> Where hope deceives, there truths die,
> keeping only *promises* of Life forever.

"Where did you learn that?" I asked.

"I made it up." Amada had been studying music, harmony and composition for years. She intended to compose songs that would make a healing impact on the consciousness. Unfortunately, Dad did not support her project graciously, so she had to do it without his knowledge. Nevertheless, her talents were beginning to flower beautifully. Soon she would be making a record, "The Seven Songs of Life."

Lakshmi, constantly traveling through her levels of awareness, had become what was called a Silent One, in alignment with her Soul's destiny. Leaving her body at rest, she would voyage in the upper realms of Light, channeling blessings of peace at different points of the world. In a way, she was a silent worker for the cause of Life.

Her wisdom had become her own sanctuary in her brain, so that she used it as a doorway to transcend the worlds. She had been reconnected with her own spiritual promise, and she often commented, "Life begins only with total realization."

One day as I sat in the hospital, I had a *deja vu* experience. I saw the beautiful scene of Lakshmi's wisdom that I had seen from outer space eons ago, after the GFH. I felt so complete. Was life a circular event, or just a dream? Were past and present alike, or did all coexist in time as one thing?

"It's all happening simultaneously," said the Cat, while I was reflecting. *"**All**, can you believe that? It's only in the understanding of the tuning of the physical instrument that you can have multisimultaneous experiences."*

"Dear Cat," I said, "since I have known you, you have been my Strength. In moments of doubt, I have rested on your soul. Even though I've learned, lived and seen — even though it seemed as if I understood the physical instrument — you still challenge me with it at the oddest moments."

"There is always another detail to find out," replied Androgynous. *"Have you seen the explanations you have gotten in school? They are true, on the level at which they are true. What's important to find out is why the Wholeness is so clear from the Soul body, why we feel in the feeling body, how we learn to think outside our Selves and how God comes together in the flesh."*

"In the flesh," I repeated. "Isn't the flesh only a vehicle?"

"Of course it's only an instrument," agreed the Cat. *"Do you know what this word means?"*

In order to find out, I stated that I did not.

"Augustus!" called the Cat. *"Come, here is coaching to be done!"*

Augustus appeared and said, *"The discovery of what an instrument is will lead us toward its function. Do you know which is the most important organ in the body?"*

The heart, I thought first. No — "The brain," I said.

"No," answered Augustus, *"but such an answer might cause you to graduate with honors in your school."*

"I will tell you a little story," said Beauty. And in her usual tender manner, she began:

"Once upon a time all the parts of the person came together to discuss which was the most important. Vested in their own arrogance, the eyes said, 'I am the most important. If I leave, you will be in the darkness — you will not be able to see your way, nor will you find your place.' And they left, leaving the person in darkness. The ears said, just as arrogantly, 'I am the connector to the sound. Without me you can't hear the voice of living entities.' And the ears left, while the body remained. One by one each organ left, each arrogantly believing it was the most important one.

"And while they were arguing," continued Beauty, *"the Breath of Life started to withdraw from the person. All the organs felt lifeless and began to cry, 'No, no, please don't go! You are indeed the most important one.'*

"This Breath of Life can be received and transcended through its receiving terminal in the brain. That is where God becomes God-man."

"Incredible!" I said. "I'll tell this story to my teachers in school!"

"No," warned Augustus, *"Don't! They'll kick you out."*

I went back to my neuroanatomy books, and saw that they presented the functions of the brain in a very primitive way. Nowhere did they mention the Breath of Life.

I wanted to know how the Breath of Life aligned the anatomy. So I centered and prayed. And this prayer came to me: "Lord of the Universe, connect and guide me to your Reality so that for the betterment of Self, I know and love and give to Self in all its forms the Truth of the Eternal One." I amazed myself by the power of my prayer. It was more than a request for shelter; it was an affirmation of faith.

There was no answer—but my whole body started to vibrate at an infinitely higher frequency, and I could perceive my brain resonating with subtle higher forces. And on my way back to school, I opened to receive the following information.

Chapter 13

Journeying with Ra

I was driving toward the golden sunset when I started feeling a tremendous heat in my face, as if I were entering the sun. My car would not go, even with my foot on the gas pedal. "Is there a spaceship nearby?" I wondered. I looked at the speedometer. Nothing registered. All the instruments were turned off.

"Press harder on the gas and start the engine again," said William. But I knew that more force would make no difference. So I relaxed, and the feeling of stuckness I'd had in my belly (where the alter ego resides) smoothed out.

"By any chance," asked the Cat, *"do you remember how this alter ego came about?"*

"Not at all," I answered. "I think I was born with it."

"Well," laughed the Cat. *"I didn't think immortal beings were ever born. Do you remember being in outer space, where there was nothing else?"*

"Sure I do," I said, deeply annoyed. I considered this an inappropriate occasion for a dialogue — my body was getting hotter and hotter, while of course the Cat, being Strength, kept cool.

"Do you remember how this alter ego came about?" he insisted.

"I do," said William, trying to help me corner my obviously forgotten memory.

"Interesting," said Augustus. *"We could all try to help you, but none of us will do it because we want to help your Ego, your I-ness, not the mask that sometimes..."*

"...covers up your Self," Androgynous said, completing the sentence.

Feeling truly honored, I said my prayer again: "Lord of the Universe, connect and guide me to your Reality so that for the betterment of Self, I know and love and give to Self in all its forms the Truth of the Eternal One."

As the temperature seemed to cool off a bit, the car started spinning into the sun.

I was twenty-one years of age. I had experienced more trials than most people my age; I had a beautiful girl friend; I had a harmonious relationship with my family; and I had an interesting career. In this spinning I felt I was going to die.

"Immortal beings die? What nonsense is this?" asked the Cat. *"Are you sure it's not your alter ego speaking?"*

"What's wrong with an alter ego?"

"It steals from your life," said the Cat.

"It's okay for sometimes, maybe for relating to things—but never for relating to people. It never comes from the heart," added Augustus.

"Do you remember," the Cat said strongly, *"when we were in outer space, and you looked into the crystal and saw the All? You asked the question, 'Why is this happening to me?' while a tear rolled from your eyes. The tears formed lakes, and in these lakes you saw an image, and then you asked, 'Why me?'*

"I told you, 'Don't ask that way.' The question was still the alter ego.

"When you got a body again, the alter ego located itself in the third wheel, the so-called wheel of movement, power and will. And sitting there it could cause you pain, because every time a thought comes over you, the alter ego contracts the wheel to meet its limited perspective and feels the need to create layers to protect you from the All."

"This is similar," added August, *"to why your father collapses in his stomach each and every time there is some stress."*

"Most of humanity is profane," the Cat went on. *"Therefore, they limit existence to the finite matters that can be perceived by the lower chakras of the body, trying to protect the Self—or what it*

imagines Self to be – and closing off to higher integrated experiences."

I felt I knew all this, but had to feel it within my Self to understand it better.

"You are experiencing Empathy," added Beauty sweetly, who in the midst of the solar light was fully merged with me. *"Empathy is a resonance that is possible only when you are aware of the ultimate purpose for Life. Unless one has this form of Love for one's Self, there can't be Love for others."*

I felt relieved. Here we are, right on course, I thought, according to the Father's Plan.

"Yes," said a voice from the center of the sun. *"I am Ra of the great Central Sun. I am the same Life Force that nourishes the bees and the plants, the insects and the animals, the cord of silver and gold, and the air in its essential manifestations of nourishing energies for all that lives. I am called* ***prana.*** *I am the same Life Force as that which you call* ***you*** *– which you are when you open up to the forms of thought that I imbue in you. I am your Self and I am all Selves; there is no distinction between us. You are now in the living room of your solar system. How do you feel?"*

"Wonderful!" I replied. In my solar plexus there was no strain. In my belly there was no interrupted breathing (which, it seemed, had been the cause of all my ills).

"Come into me," said Ra, *"and I will show you a different perspective. It is by Becoming that one truly lives. Then when you return to Tria Ra, you will think about what you have seen here. As your understanding in the human frame grows, you will become lighter and everyone around you will be attracted by the Light-ness of your Self."*

I stepped out of my body to merge with Ra.

"Look," said Ra, as I was feeling the Light-ness of my Soul, *"we will take a journey through this body, which you have termed an 'investment' or 'vehicle,' and enter a human cell."*

We projected ourselves into a cell in the bloodstream. It felt like landing on a planet that was traveling in space; we saw other cells in the distance.

"Incredible!" I said. "This is like being in outer space!"

"In this case, it's inner space," replied Ra. *"but let's continue."* Traveling through the wall of the cell, we entered the cytoplasmic zone. This was a universe of its own. We traveled through various mitochondrial lisosomes, which penetrated their own membranes in order to enter new worlds even more expansive in magnitude and more precise in their operations.

We journeyed through the organelle level, the first structure, and then deeper into molecules, atoms, ions and universes of subatomic paraphysical energetic particles, until we arrived at an electric generator. This, infinite in itself, was being nourished by the Light to produce energy to keep the entire operation functioning.

"Lots of water," said Ra. *"The body is mainly made of water so it can conduct the electricity of the Light. It is I, the Light, that vibrate this universe into alignment. Now do you know which is the most important organ in the body?"*

"All," I said. "Or — no, the Light."

"Indeed," Ra answered, *"when all organs leave, then the Light remains — You Are. When the Light leaves, nothing Is. Now,"* it added, as we were once again outside the cell and organs of the body, *"this whole system is regulated by a thought of Who one Is. Thought, conducting the energy-in-motion that takes the form of Light, tunes the body by entering the central programming unit (CPU) in the brain through what is called the seventh wheel.*

"The brain," continued Ra, as we entered the brain's enormous machinery, *"is the only standard piece in the human body — the part that doesn't change. Unlike other cells, it doesn't ordinarily reproduce itself under third-dimensional conditions. When a cell in the brain gets out of shape, its function can't be replaced by Will.*

"It is the central unity; therefore it lies protected within the skull, atop the upright human body so that other animals can't get to it. Even if they did, the skull would protect the brain.

"Medical people like yourself do not comprehend the brain — they cut it, and it dissolves. Because it's so watery, all it does well is transduce the energy of Light and empower the rest of the wheels to give the Light frequencies to all the other organs — in short, it psychosynergizes the whole system."

"Psychosynergizes?" I asked.

"Yes, it aligns all the energies that come from the Soul by receiving them and referring them, in synergetic alignment, to the other wheels, tuning them to the frequencies the organs need in order to operate."

"So the brain is just a big receiver?"

"And a transmitter of impulses in perfect alignment with the racial plan for evolution," answered Ra. *"The Light enters and the hypothalamic wheel — the hypothalamus — starts the operation. That is why a certain tradition called it 'the thousand-petaled lotus': It's like a lotus that's open to the sun and receives Light, which goes through the systems of the body.*

"Now," added Ra, *"when this Light must filter through the alter ego, only limited thoughts can enter, and then Who You Are is out of touch with your own body. Therefore this alter ego alternates the current that the true Ego sends forth. When this happens, some circuits get disconnected and the energy reverberates into a peripheral plane around the body. This is the astral plane. There, energy fields that can enter the body take on a sort of life of their own, creating what the ancients called demons, and what we have named Imago.*

"I am not talking of positive imagination, which empowers human actions. I am talking of the imaginary magnetic fields that make man fearful, hurt and think himself to be in danger.

"There the alter ego takes full charge and the organs of the body, not receiving the expanded vision of their function, go out of psychosynergy, thus running amok.

"When they are out of alignment, some cells (which, as you have seen, are universes in themselves) stop producing and atrophy. Others — believing in their cell memory that they need to work more because the supply is shortened — reproduce themselves, causing growth that you have termed cancer."

"I can see a similarity between this and the structure of society," I said reflectively.

"Indeed, how do you see that?"

I started to explain to Ra how, by the lack of purpose, the social alter ego had taken over on earth and how now on Tria Ra false values ruled the scene. How some societies were perishing and others were living according to Imago, not according to their essential substance. How other groups were metastasizing —expanding imperialistically—to take over other regions in the world. And how all this was happening because the machinery seemed to be in danger, and so the alter ego thought it needed to protect itself.

"Exactly," said Ra. *"The more you think bigger thoughts – the more you expand your perspective of Wholeness – the more I can enter the body through the seventh wheel and align the whole system in joy and harmony once again."*

"So," I asked, "do you think I should tell this in medical school?"

"You can even tell it in your life."

This was the tuning of the physical instrument.

~ ❧ ~

I returned to my body and told the Cat, "I'm satisfied. Now it makes total sense."

"I'm glad," he replied. *"But watch your driving. You almost hit that tree."*

Chapter 14

Moving Outward

Finally understanding the brain enlightened me and allowed me to more clearly accept being in the body.

"*Being* in the body?" asked Amada, surprised. "What do you mean by that? *Using* is all I thought of — and enjoying it."

I tried to convey to her the magnificence that I had experienced in each cell. "Amada," I said, "there is no difference — 'as above, so below.' This saying is true. I am experiencing so much love and enjoyment right here on this plane."

"Then you will become attached to it again and miss it when you don't have it," she chided.

"I can take it with me — to any dimension," I asserted, not truly knowing where this statement had come from.

"Nonsense," said Amada.

"What does it matter whether she understands," asked Androgynous, *"if you now can live your truth?"*

"But I would like to share, or at least talk with others to find out if someone else knows. It's really hard to have a dialogue with my professors in med school."

"Indeed," said the Cat. *"They are set in their labeling and categorizing. I am not saying they are not efficient, even helpful at times in what they do. But they are as stuck in their mental categories as patients are stuck in their pain."*

"Cat," I said, "you know I spend extra hours in the hospitals talking with patients about what they really feel. Many times they get confused about their pain, and even let it go. Yesterday, a man who couldn't move his legs for years started dancing — but this morning his attendant was mad at him for leaving his bed! If the Soul's thought commanded the Light through the brain to move his legs, what was there to get mad about?"

"Remember the conversation about the alter ego," said the Cat. *"The relationship that is established between the doctor and the patient occurs between their alter egos. So one takes possession of the doctor's role and the other takes the patient's role. And they protect each other by holding these roles in place. In the doctor's alter ego there is noplace for hope for so-called miracles. But when the Spirit activates its Self in the body, it is the Ego that commands – and thus the man can move."*

"So," I said, "as the doctor, I facilitated the Spirit to be in charge."

"Of course. But now the person needs to be reinforced and educated. The longer he has been rewarded to protect his alter ego, the longer it will take for his Self to stay in command. The tuning of the physical instrument, as we used to call it, is therefore the tuning of the Self in man."

"Then how does one get rid of the alter ego?" I asked.

"Hmm – that is a difficult question," confessed the Cat. *"I don't have one, so I don't really know."*

(As I later found out through what I termed my 'spiritual search,' that *was* a difficult question.

Now I asked, "How does one fight what does not exist?"

"Be at peace," said the Cat. *"It's time to return to your hospital."*

~ ❧ ~

I immersed myself in my last year of studies, trying to put aside the conflict between my real knowledge and the knowledge required by the tests at school. I probably would have never passed and graduated had I not kept the two sets of data from intermingling. I learned what they wanted me to learn in school. In fact, medical school was very easy.

So I took some classes in philosophy to see if the philosophers could help me reason. I didn't last too long there; I soon discovered that the teachers were more concerned with analyzing how certain thinkers thought than in thinking newly with us. Alter ego prevailed there also; and the laws of currency, which were similar to those on earth, offered these teachers a salary to maintain the status quo and not to question what was beneath the surface.

My search now took a new form. I wanted to find out if there were others who knew what I knew, and whether the teachers of these systems were truly immersed in what they were teaching or whether they were just acting the part.

"I question everything and everyone," I declared in a political school assembly, "about your true intention to be here!" They all clapped, which greatly surprised me. I had expected them to react angrily to my questioning, but it seemed that somewhere inside, human beings know the Truth, and in their depths they want the question that will bring forth the Truth.

"Watch it," said Cat. *"Alter ego controls this world. You will be endangering yourself if you don't adapt or take a stand for declaring Who You Truly Are and bring about the seeds of a new civilization."*

Lakshmi begged me to stay out of politics. So I did, even though my social concerns had moved away from my individual need to be with the suffering and expand toward a larger sphere.

I had clearly seen the lack of synergy in bodies that were not aligned with the purpose of their life. All of society was a body at large. This body didn't love itself, because the single individuals didn't love them Selves.

Once I spoke to people of Love. But their response was only, "Oh, you are so young that you can't get your mind off sex."

"Sex!" I said, now realizing that in our culture Love and sex were seen as the same thing. This was an entry point for the actions of Imago, who through the dark forces attempted to avoid the Ascension of beings and the descension of the true Light of Spirit.

That day I decided to go into seclusion. I needed time and space for myself. "I still can't transmit all that I have experienced," I told my mother. "Either I or society or both aren't ready yet. I vow that I'll find a better way to serve!"

Thus I dove into myriad adventures, which lasted many

seasons. I had my own mastery, but I couldn't reason it out. At twenty-three I needed to find out and make all the necessary errors.

"No one comes in the flesh without erring," said Augustus. *"Do you remember when we met? I told you I had erred several times before I gained the blue pearl, which now belongs to you.*

"We live out a pattern of life, and all of humanity goes toward annihilation over and over again."

I didn't want to think about that, but now — when things fall at their own gravity — I couldn't avoid it anymore.

"I need to learn to live in this world," I told my family. "My inner space is safe within me, and before I let it out I'll explore this world."

"I'm afraid for you," worried Lakshmi. "It seems you're leaving home."

"No, mother — I *am* at home. I'm like a turtle whose home goes wherever it goes. I must explore the romantic end of this saga. I have to tell you I am now in love."

"What happened to Bhakti-Shadai?" asked Amada.

"I love her also. But this is a different kind of love." I hadn't told anybody about the woman I had met on the street. It broke all rules: She was married and had a child, and she left her husband and went with me. She was my first teacher on Tria Ra. She taught me a great love.

> I'll tell you
> what the silence of a green field means,
> where nothing can reach you except
> what really deserves to reach you:
> equilibrium,
> tranquility in an ocean of communication,
> peace;
> that soft tender caress that we can feel
> only when we are open to it.
>
> The singing of the birds had a message
> of sweetness and Love and Life:
> Life itself was grasped and given
> in a supreme ecstatic loving.

This wasn't only a theoretical communication –
it was a vibration in unison between an I and a Thou,
a call in the silence,
one's own salvation,
an abundant giving and receiving –
but *from* one's Self, not *because of* one's Self.

Nothing between you and I was planned
or preestablished.
This adventure toward living
was Life itself –
not for life, not for anything;
it simply Was.
or you either.
It was the glory of intangibility.

That night was beautiful;
a fresh wind was whispering, not too strongly,
the sea was dark
and your vivid memory evoked my love.
It wasn't a common love –
it was a birth,
a letting go of part of my Self
to become One with the night
that would strengthen me
till the next day.
Then you will see awakening.

PART III

COMPLETION

Chapter 1

The Journey

"Once again I am a doctor, as I have been in many lifetimes, on many planets. I know my secret—but I need to do more research. That way, when I use my knowledge it will truly be complete," I thought.

"Yes," agreed the Cat, my constant companion who supported me strongly in my new endeavors.

"But," added Augustus, *"don't deny the help you already can give along the way."*

Beauty said, *"You will experience situations that will attempt to make you forget Who You Are. But remember that you'll come out all right."*

"There is nothing to fear. I'm with you," said Androgynous, *"and the journey you have chosen to embark on is the next stage of preparation for mastering all that is a barrier for the Soul on the material plane."*

"Remember," Augustus reminded, *"errors don't exist—we only call them that. Actually, calling them errors reflects our feelings about ourselves. These* **feelings** *are enemies to be overcome."*

"Now you don't have them," the Diamond told me. *"You are clear, and you see."*

"But," said Will, *"in order to master your Self, you will be given tests. You will be able to help others only in those things that you have mastered yourself. This process goes on for almost twice as long as your current age, by which time you will have reached full maturity. Then and only then will you be fully satisfied."*

"I don't really know what I'm getting into," I confessed. "The crossroads I saw were much simpler than all this talk."

"Courage," advised the Cat. *"Listen to your Self—you who have been One with All; you who on rockets blew planets apart; you who left the Council of Twelve; you who survived the great explosion on earth. You now hesitate and are afraid. Shame on you! Remember Who You Are."*

I looked into the Cat's eyes, and the strength of its Essence empowered me once again. "But," I protested nevertheless, "I don't see the point. Why leave the balance point, I Am, to go into adventures that are full of risks?"

"Do you feel danger now?" asked the Cat. *"Good, this medicine is working. It's easy to know everything when you're in a sheltered home—and, as you told your mother, Tria Ra is your home."*

"Building a character is not an easy task," said Authenticity.

All the known qualities of Essence were present in this Council of my Essence—Will, Strength, Beauty, Certainty, Clarity, Wisdom, Truth, Authenticity, Compassion, Forgiveness, Spirit, Love—and the totality of it, the Essence of my true Being, Universal Consciousness.

And then a Light filled the room. It was similar to, yet more powerful than, the whirling light than came from the spaceships that night on the beach with Laila. The Light was more powerful than the one that connected my thoughts to my brain and triggered the electricity throughout my body. It was even stronger than the one I had seen in Source.

"I Am the Light of God; I am the Spirit that you are," it said. *"I am also a quality of Essence; I preside over this Council of Twelve in your name until you learn the task of life."*

I stood in the center of my own etheric robe, and the Light filled me, surrounded me and protected me throughout all the layers of my Self—through my thought and feeling bodies as well as through my physical body, interpenetrating it in such a wholesome way that I felt fully attuned. This Council of Twelve, the cosmic individualities of my Being, surrounded me. In my heart was the emerald of Truth; in my belly was the ruby of Strength, curled up beautifully.

And William, holding the crystal out in front of me (where the alter ego had been living), designed a crystal crown in which to hold the gems: the aquamarine Beauty at my left, the blue pearl of Wisdom in my head, and the diamond of Clarity between my eyes. The blue sapphire of Compassion and the stardust of Forgiveness were at each side; the silver sword of Authenticity was at my feet; and the Purple Rose of Spirit enveloped me, while golden Love filled and connected me with the Oneness of my Self.

"This," said the Light, *"is the tuning of the physical instrument. Now your first lesson is to go to a desert and find the angels for your body."*

"The angels for my body in the desert?" I asked.

But I was back in my living room, with a deeper certainty in my heart.

Chapter 2

In the Desert

After entering the school, I was sent by my teacher to a lonely place — the interior of the driest desert of the planet.

Days went by and nothing happened. I sat and contemplated the nothingness — the vastness of the sand, just sand. There was no one, not even a desert rat. It was hot during the day and cold at night.

I had been instructed not to call on the qualities of Essence. They had said, *"What you know and already have can't be taken away if it's really yours. So don't rely on it."*

I saw what alter ego is: It is nothing but a compressed way of being. It blocks the receptivity of thought (which enters my brain in the form of Light) into a collapsed interpretation of life. In that interpretation, it believes life separates itself from itself.

It was waiting for something to occur.

So was I.

"It's lovely to be alone," I said to myself, without the presence of the Cat.

But even naming my aloneness didn't make a change. My commitment was to be by my Self.

Days went by, and at first they were very easy to count. But after awhile there was no way to keep track. The situation grew more uncomfortable.

I had only a limited amount of food and water with me, and I started to worry. But my concern did not produce a change. Nothing produced a change. Sometimes there was a wind or a sandstorm, but this was not the kind of change I needed. Or so I thought.

One morning I woke up with no hope at all. "This is my life, this is my existence," I concluded. "There is nothing to be done. Here I am now."

I looked far into the desert, and as far as I could see it was all alike. Sand, sand and more sand. Hot days, cold nights.

I started to think, to remember all my lifetimes. But none of them — what this one had been, what that one had been — meant too much right then. I gave myself courage by telling myself that this was only a school assignment — "But what school?" I asked myself at once. "That was one kind of school, but what kind is this?"

I cried, "I expect realization!" But I didn't break my promise. I had said I would use no magic at all. That included not invoking Who I Am. "Why, if I Am What I Am?" I asked my Self. "Because I said so!" I answered bluntly. "This is a time of being in the desert."

How tricky the mind is, saying "this is a time," as if to shorten it. I felt like I was going out of my mind. It was like checkmating myself to test my Being, regardless of circumstance, location or environment.

"Yes, but this is awful" (when I interpret it as such).

I decided to sit and meditate. "On what?" I asked myself. Both on earth and Tria Ra teachers gave their disciples either words or symbols on which to concentrate. The disciples would repeat these words, inducing a hypnotic state. Then they could easily be pacified and tuned by their teacher's will. Not that the teacher wanted to control them. This will was to produce enlightenment. Yet the teacher's will was not the disciple's will.

"Or they could concentrate on a flower," I commented to myself. "But this desert doesn't have even one flower!"

I decided to sit down — to just sit there.

The mind in this human form is amazing, I discovered. It's like a monkey, jumping from here to there, trying to grasp something — a thought, a word, a feeling, an idea. Eventually it seizes on actions to perform, people to talk to, places to go.

Anything but being still.

"I need to still this mind," said the mind. Or maybe it was I who said this, since by now I had everything all confused.

"Sh sh, sh," I answered myself. I liked this repetition of words — "Sh, sh." It was like a very calming mantra. Obviously, it was the most well-known mantra in the universe. We all had been hypnotized thus — "sh, sh" — when our mothers attempted to pacify us. And then, whether angrily or nicely, we would invoke it for one another.

So I stopped — I had promised not to use mantras, either. Nor could I count sheep, another repetition humans use in an attempt to still the mind when going to sleep. "Dammit!" I complained. "What *can* I do?"

All seemed to be technique. And I had thought I knew the natural state of man.

"I know the divine state of Soul when it is fully filled with Spirit," I reminded my Self. "Yes," I countered, "but with all I know about it, how come I am not still?"

Not being allowed to pray, chant or meditate; not finding any action with which to engage myself; and having promised not to engage with the Council of Essence, outer space was my only hope. I had made no promise about refraining from this aspect. But no spaceship ever showed up.

There was no tree — noplace to seek my friends, the elves and gnomes. There was no water in which to find fish or dolphins with whom to relate.

All — family, lovers, friends — was just a picture in my mind. There was nobody and nothing.

In this staleness (as I saw it) my life was passing by. The days were long — I walked little, just sat — and I found no end to them. My beard was growing and my sunburnt face was getting dry. I saw no point in living any longer, yet there was no point in taking my life, either. There was only one extraordinary thing: The amount of my small food and water supply always remained the same.

I had given up attachments to my thoughts, memories and such. And a new kind of emptiness started to occupy my inner space. It was like voiding myself of everything; there was nothing to hold onto. Yet as this was taking place, my body was coming more and more alive.

"A curious paradox," I told my Self. "The less I do or feel or think or even remember, the more energy my muscles seem to have. What for?" I didn't know. But with more energy, I had less desire to sleep.

Now the days were even longer.

I noticed I wanted the days to go by fast so that it would be night sooner; but when it was night I wished for the sun to rise. "I see I have no choice at all," I said, and I let my Self go. I screamed and yelled; I ate the sand. And when I realized that I had no say over where I was and how long I would be here, I experienced madness — and rapture.

After my irate attack on my Self, I felt more empty than I ever had. For days I walked around like a zombie.

I created ties with an area of sand, which I called "home." Then I left home — the whole desert was my home. For days I didn't eat or drink. I seemed to have no needs at all. I collapsed and fainted.

When I regained consciousness, I felt a tingling in my hands and feet. It was a very circumscribed feeling, one that communicated some thoughts.

"We are your goals," I heard. *"It is in our custody that your objectives will be achieved."*

"What?" I exclaimed. Certainly, the heat and dehydration had driven me insane — now I was hallucinating!

"And we," tingled the forearms and legs, *"are the instruments for achieving your goals."*

Oh no, I thought, now each part of the body is falling apart. I must truly be dead!

"And we," continued the knees and elbows, *"are the style in which your instruments behave."*

"The capacity of all your actions resides in us," the arms and thighs vibrated in a deep voice.

Both my lower and upper extremities had become enlivened. But the survival of the rest of the body — which I identified with as myself — was truly endangered. The sun was so strong that I couldn't even keep my eyes open for the rest of the speaking. I felt and heard only my gender speak: *"I orient you where to go. If you follow me, survival is a guarantee."*

In my abdomen, all the intestines came alive and resonated with my kidneys to a rhythmic harmony. *"We are the ones who eliminate all the toxins you create. We are always serving you; it doesn't matter what you do."* While my intestines worked away the little I had eaten during my desert diet, they sang a continuous melody:

Don't misunderstand at all.
We eliminate also what comes from the Soul,
all the things you do not need
while your ego sits in greed.
We let go and clean you up,
releasing images that sap the energy of Self.

"Oh," I said, "so elimination is not just physical — it also clears up all excess. Good!" My dramatic outlook on desert life was being cleansed, and I started to regain a method for being present.

"I am that method," said the liver, organizing the body's processing factory in a methodical way.

I felt inspired and took a deep breath. The hot desert air entered my nostrils, went down my throat, passed through the trachea and bronchia to the lungs, entered the alveoli, and released toxic waste through the breath.

"See?" these organs said. *"We are the organs of respiration, ventilation, cleansing and exchange. We are here to make possible anything you are inspired toward."*

They were overwhelmed by a powerful beat from the heart: *"I am the impulse that guides you around — I circulate nourishment while leading your way. I serve you obediently and never judge your footsteps. I give you the impulse to go in the direction you say you want to go."*

Want to go or *need* to go? I reflected, coming more and more awake.

My lips were dry, and so was my mouth. This feeling of dryness had reached my stomach. *"We need water,"* they all said.

"If you would just pay attention to us, we would inform you of what you need. You need water!" So I made finding water my objective. My legs carried me where my orientation guided me, and there I found a spring. "Thank you," I said, not knowing whom to address.

"It was I who saw the spring," said the eyes. *"I am the vision of the form."*

"While I am the substance of this life," said the logos in the inner ear.

Then all said together, *"We're the twelve angels of your body. We mentate — think — for you, so you don't have to think for us. We are in perfect alignment. Now it's time to listen to us."*

I spent the next days in the desert in total harmony. Each of my twelve angels, functioning cooperatively with the others, moved me, fed me and organized my life.

The desert had become a home. I had no thought of ever leaving.

Chapter 3

In the Midst of Humankind

I found myself walking in the streets of a populated Tria Ra city.

"Who do you think you are!" the people asked me angrily. "Don't you have better ways to dress!?"

"Excuse me," I said, seeing my image reflected in a window of a fashionable men's clothing store. It was virtually wild. I was barefoot, and I looked as if I had not shaved in years, nor washed my body or my torn shirt and pants.

"Outrageous...insolent bastard...filthy...dirty...!" These and other deprecations were hurled at me.

The voice of the Master of the School said, *"You said the desert felt like home. So now you are home again You were to receive a teaching in the* ***midst*** *of humankind."*

It wasn't until the angels had manifested in my body that I had regained my sense of Self. Now, with this sense regained and with my promise not to call forth the powers within still intact, I was in the city.

For so many nights during my desert retreat, I had thought of man and woman with nostalgic feelings. But here no one cared to have me close. People found my appearance utterly disgusting. The most heartfelt statements I heard were full of pity. "How low can a man degrade?" said a pastor, walking by, avoiding my eyes. I felt sadness for him – his mind was lying. I wanted to ask him to practice what he preached; but as I approached he ran away.

Women who once would have admired my appearance now shunned me. "No one sees Who I Am," I realized. "Only masks walk around, and this time my mask isn't pleasing." My years in the desert had taken their toll on my appearance, even though I was still young.

"Can you tell me where I can wash myself?" I asked a youth who seemed open and quite bright.

But he responded, "Hush, go away from me, you dog! Didn't your parents teach you to wash yourself?"

I smelled foul; I looked disastrous. Yet my angels were with me.

The heart spoke: *"Now you know that all is invisible to the naked eye."*

The ear said, *"Rejoice in the sound with which they speak. Even if the content of their words seems against you, the sound of Life is still the same."*

"Don't judge," said the methodical liver. *"Even if everyone judges you, you still don't need to judge them."*

"Just watch," said the eyes. *"Watch the form and listen for where they are coming from."*

The voice of the Master added, *"You, a man on earth, are just like them. Each and every one is you, and all the ways they talk reflect their personality. But they are not their personality. That's only the mask, which they wear with one purpose only: to teach you understanding."*

I was tired and confused. "Now I wish I were back in the desert. At least it was quiet there."

*"You **are** in the desert,"* answered the voice. *"It's **all** desert. The whole universe is void of Soul where Souls have covered themselves up."*

"But in the desert there was no one," I insisted.

*"And here there is also no one. And that's the problem. When there is **One**, harmony prevails. Are you at one with yourself?"*

"What a journey!" I said. "And this is supposed to teach me life!"

*"This **is** life,"* came the answer. *"It is easy to be enlightened when you are sheltered. Now you are exposed."*

"How long is this going to take?" I insisted. In answer, a whirling twelve-pointed star appeared in front of us. It looked like a hologram. "What is this?" I asked.

From the center of the star the voice continued talking: *"Through this star you must learn to see me through them all."*

"Them all?" I asked.

"Yes. You have seen the different responses that people had to your form — some spit at you, some threw stones, some insulted you, some turned slightly away, some resented your presence next to their store, and so on. The image you currently project makes you a threat to them. And yet I am in them, the same as in you. How did you feel when they judged you?"

"Unappreciated," I responded.

"And are you the filth and dirt and murk they see?"

"No!" I answered. "I still Am my Self."

"Then if I Am in you, you have an advantage over them, because you know and they forgot. Therefore they react to you in terms of the way they learned to be."

"But I have done nothing wrong to them," I complained. "It seems they saw me through their eyes and hated me. It's unfair."

"Can you feel for them? How much suffering and pain they must endure when they see you and your angels as murk and dirt!"

"I am lonely," I exclaimed. "When I was in the desert with the sand, of course there was no one to speak to — but *here*...!"

"There is no one to speak to, indeed," said the voice. *"I'll tell you why: When a man is born through the birth canal, he forgets himself. As that happens, he feels afraid and covers himself with a mask. Through this mask he forgets his nature even more, covering him Self deeper still. This forces him to find a thicker mask..."*

"...and so on," I added. "It seems like a vicious circle."

"It is indeed. Therefore, man is born in a fixation. This is the key to his realization. If he learns to see the Soul, he becomes a master of his own. If he learns to become Spirit, he is one with the Lord of the Universe."

"Wow!" I said. "So there are twelve major fixations, and you are always behind this star. And people respond to me not according to who I am, but according to their fixation."

"Now you are catching on. What you need to learn is to hear

my voice behind the masks of men. No matter how they speak to me – no matter what they do to you."

"Seems hard," I said.

"It **is** *hard – when you are wearing your mask, which you do each time you identify with your fixations. Everyone has them all, although some are more immersed in one than the others."*

"And there are twelve?" I asked. "Same as the Council...?"

"Remember, you are not supposed to use any information from before."

"Why not?" I asked. "It would be of help."

"There **are** *no whys, and we need no help. We want* **certainty,***"* said the Master harshly. *"And in certainty there is nothing else."*

What a tremendous ability I have to create trouble for myself, I thought. With all my experiences, what did I join the School for?

"To master yourself," answered the voice. *"When you master your Self, you fulfill the purpose of your life. That starts the clarity of the Mission. We thought you were interested! Would you like us to dismiss you now in the midst of your training? You could become a paid worker in your local hospital, and help people to anesthetize themselves,"* the voice said cynically. *"Who wants cosmic consciousness, anyway?"*

"No!" I screamed. I abhorred the idea of mediocrity. I remembered how hospitals did implantations on people's thoughts to discourage them from discovering themselves. Not only was it false, but it also hurt. I decided to commit myself to the path I was on. "Advance," I said, "and forward. I don't want to go anywhere else. No matter what it takes, let us move on."

~ ❧ ~

In this city there was a central park. Across from the park were assembly halls where people from all places came together to discuss the state of Tria Ra's affairs. The voice commanded me to be a beggar in the park. As a beggar my appearance would be accepted, and I would have a place from which to see the twelve ways in which man forgets himself.

I did this for many years, and I observed this Self-forgetting thousands of times — the myriad examples of the twelve ways in which these people were not in touch with the nature of the heart. A typical instance went like this.

Chapter 4

The Assembly of the Empties

As I approached the assembly, I felt a sense of emptiness. It was a strange sensation, and it emanated from the twelve characters who had met to discuss survival on Tria Ra.

At this time Tria Ra was undergoing political upheaval. There was famine, war, strikes, unemployment, inflation and forgetfulness of the Purpose of life. This disconnection from the Spirit's guidance was creating a series of blunders in human interaction.

All this reminded me of earth.

The emptiness here was so obvious that it had created an experiential black hole which in itself sapped energy, even from the plants in the park. This was a sadder view of the collapse of civilization.

"Who has allowed the presence of this distasteful being in our midst!" sneered a haughty, proud woman. "Are we to tolerate such a dirty slob in this most distinguished court of superior elegance in which the destiny of the world is being discussed?"

"Who cares?" the older man said passively, in a patterned laziness. His indolent ways had kept him going through many assemblies in which nothing was resolved. "Who cares if we are getting nowhere, anyway?"

"I do, I do! Not only about him but also about the efficiency of this meeting!" lied a young executive — who, evidently, was more concerned with his own vain image in the group than with any substantial issue to be furthered.

"The situation of the world is dreadful!" exclaimed a member in the shadows. "I am afraid we won't survive. And all of you, I accuse, really are doing nothing for salvation!" His eyes were covered by thick glasses, and in his fear he mostly addressed the wall, since he was unable to confront the other members face to face.

"I am disappointed that this meeting is not going anywhere," declared a tight-lipped man angrily. "I recall that this has happened before, and it is not worth my time to be with all of you. I resent you, and I resent myself for being here. I should have known better and stayed home!" He represented the kingdom of disdain. All his life he had suffered from the inner revolution of his own organs. He was so full of resentment that his face was full of boils and pus was flowing from his face.

"I am scared," insisted the one with thick glasses. "It looks to me..."

"Shut up, all of you shut up!" growled a bully, who wanted revenge. "If *I* control the world, *then* we will have peace!"

"Sure," said the flatterer. "But who wants your kind of peace?"

"Who cares, who cares, who cares," moaned a member who had lost his balance. "I am feeling depressed. Hopelessness prevails, and we cannot agree. We all say we want to have peace, but we don't even speak the same language."

"I plan to propose a common language," interjected a skinny, gluttonous man who simultaneously was eating, drinking, reading, taking notes and trying to speak.

"He knows nothing," grumbled a miser in the corner. "No one knows anything. I know, but am not ready to say."

"I hate you all!" hissed a fierce woman. "I don't know why, but hate prevails in me. I think the best that could happen would be the annihilation of this meeting – and probably the world!" she screamed, spitting venom.

"Now it's hopeless," an old man added weakly. "It's all out in the open and we can't agree."

This assembly has failed, I thought. The representatives would go back to their countries all stuck in their own viewpoints, and probably have wars. It seemed so much like how they treated me when I first came back from the desert. Even though it looked as if they were talking to each other, they were just talking to themselves. Actually, *all* they were talking about was themselves.

As I was walking out, I saw the twelfth member — the greedy one — selling assembly T-shirts, souvenirs, postcards — anything that might make him a buck. He had totally forgotten the reason for being there.

What a lesson! During this meeting I had completely forgotten that these people were human Souls. Their masks and ways of being were so solidly attached to their selves that their emptiness — which I had felt earlier and which matched their own emptiness — solidified the appearance of their role. Spirit watched, removed, as the dark forces ruled their lives just as they ruled the lives of others.

I had watched all the qualities of passion through which they suffered. All were new to me, and in their brief meeting I could see the workings of the whole material plane. But since my seventh wheel was functioning healthily, I did not judge them. Nor did I judge myself for having judged before. All these passions were qualities that prevailed out of Self-forgetfulness — being afraid, and covering it up.

Fear, planning, withdrawing and greed were attributes of the inability to feel safe and of not knowing what to do. Obviously, with this background any action became Self-protective, thus misunderstanding the Self (who was Self-forgotten).

Naturally, those who did not even recall their Being were lazy about living, and overcompensated for this laziness with lots of busy activity such as the building of weapons; and vengeance, resentment and hatred were a compensation for not being one's Self. Under such conditions, who could blame those who chose to die? Obviously, the weaker their life became the more arrogant or sad they were.

I reported to the Master: "I have not seen any other way for interactions in *this* desert to occur, when there is no knowledge of the Soul."

"Indeed," said the Master's voice. *"And all these attributes impede the ability to move on consciously. It is like a hydra with twelve heads. Even had you lived in this world for many years, I doubt that you would have seen the interactive level at which humans live. If they have a higher goal or purpose, all that happens takes place in a lifetime. But when they don't have a higher goal, they become this one passion, and only one — and even though they touch the many, they hold as friends only those who are just like them or only slightly different."*

"Isn't this even more isolated than the desert?" I asked. "There I felt loneliness at first, then aloneness and space. But after years of solitude, these twelve devils — which were in *me*, too — finally left."

"That is why you were brought back to the city — to see yourself interact in life. This is also a desert, the desert of human isolation. I recommend that you read your notes on the passions again."

I did so, many times. And just recalling my observations awakened my understanding of limited fixations. Since I still was learning at this School, I kept my promise not to use any magic with my Self. Therefore, in my daily observations at the park, I suffered when I saw adults quarreling about what appeared to be objective matters but was really a projection of their own fixated way of being alive.

"How can one get rid of this?" I asked the voice.

"Awareness," said the Master. *"Awareness is like Light. It is Light."*

The more I saw it, the more I could see it.

I could see the negative love that children received from their parents. They didn't stand a chance — either they were like their parents to please them, or they were their opposite. And all to gain their attention, which they called love. But very little Love flowed through these lives. These people were more or less stagnant in their mechanism, swearing they were right, making others wrong, and rarely reaching an understanding of themselves. The most evolved ones would say, "I accept myself — this is the way I am, take it or leave it," never even imagining that there was a way to truly Be.

People who engaged in learning about themselves analyzed how they were, or tried to exchange it for another "better" way.

Year by year different masks were made available. But Essence rarely was mentioned.

"After years of desert life this is invaluable," I told the Master. "Thank you so much. Now I must go back home."

"Home," said the voice, *"is your destiny. Now,"* he added, *"we'll send you to another school."*

"Another school!" I cried. "Does this training ever end?"

"Mine hasn't," replied the Master, *"and I'm as old as Life."*

"Farewell," I said, "and thank you." And I walked toward the closest airport to take a plane to the ocean.

Chapter 5

Oceana

My plane was descending toward Oceana. "How exciting!" I told myself. After all my desert experiences, I was ready for some romance. Or so I thought.

Oceana was a small community with a beautiful beach surrounded by coconut trees. There were magnificent villas built by the citizens during times of affluence. Today they were used as boarding homes, bed-and-breakfast places, or furnished apartments for young professionals.

I remembered that a friend from medical school lived nearby. Raz was Joe's brother (Joe was the high school companion who never spoke to me after the night in the forest with the pumas). Raz and I had become friends during our year of internship. So now I called him up, and he invited me over.

"Hakim Haiam!" he said, opening his door. "Welcome to my house. Please stay as long as you like and enjoy Oceana. How are Amada and your parents?" he asked politely.

"Fine," I said, "Fine." In truth, I had almost forgotten their existence; and as far as my name was concerned, eons had gone by since I had last heard it. "Fine, Raz," I went on, "and how are you?"

"Great. I can't wait for you to meet my fiancee — she is a beautiful nurse."

Nurses, beauties, women — I felt so alien to this world.

At the beginning of my stay with Raz, I tried to explain about the power of being able to distinguish egotypes (those qualities of passion that I had learned about in the desert). But soon I gave up. "Haiam," he said, "you complicate your life too much. Just enjoy and have a good time. That's what I do — a little work, a little play, a little fun."

"What about yourself?" I inquired. "I mean, Self?"

"This *is* myself — a little work, a little play, a little fun. I've fallen in love three times a year for the past five years. When I get bored, I change partners. No problem — nothing to complain about. Medicine gives me good money, and that's how I live my life."

He sounded cheerful. His description didn't sound bad. So I decided to stay in Oceana for awhile.

The beach, drinks and yachts were entertaining — to a point. But the point was that there was nothing nourishing for the Soul. It was nothing like the desert here — it was fun, and people even called it "light." But how far removed it was from understanding the Self.

Everything we did was for sensory stimulation. Like Raz, I changed girlfriends many times, as they exchanged me for other men. This was the kingdom of superficiality; people's lives lacked profundity, depth. I joined in drugs, dope, sex, yachting, sailing, swimming. I got a job at the clinic where Raz worked, but I rarely spent time in my office. Mostly it was closed.

After a few months of living like this, I noticed the effects of my lifestyle on my system. My face was puffed up; I had gained weight; my skin was dried out by the sun.

Raz had a girlfriend called Nina, a perfect mate for him. She dared to do what he didn't, and he admired her for that. One day Nina and Raz looked at me in surprise. "What's happening?" Nina asked. "You look tired. Sit and have a drink."

"I don't want a drink," I responded, annoyed with myself for having stayed so long.

"Call a girl and have some sex," Nina insisted, handing me the phone.

"No!" I said angrily, slamming the phone to the floor. "Leave me alone!"

I went into the other room. Both of them followed me. "Can we be of help?" they asked.

"No," I said. "I apologize. I don't feel well." It was like being in the midst of the assembly of the empties for months. Only here, the emptiness had been covered up by games. These games even disguised the basic patterns of fixation. Everything was anesthetized. Everything was "fine" — the same "fine" that had come out of me when they'd asked about my folks.

"I can't live like this," I said. "I'm sorry."

"I've given you all I've got," said Raz disappointedly. "Maybe you want some coke?"

That was the last thing I needed. Raz was using cocaine daily. Being a doctor, he obtained it with ease. The whole planet was also using cocaine in epidemic proportions. Because people were unable to confront their lives, they spent their earnings to alter their minds toward "fun" — controlling their thoughts, feeling new sensations, or enhancing their sex life.

~ ❧ ~

I had promised to use no special powers to help myself, but I thought of breaking this vow. I isolated myself for some time to pray, chant, sing, meditate, and even tell myself the story of my life. I practiced yoga standing on my head; I did t'ai chi. I danced through the waves, I ran, jumped and sang, and prayed again; but the integrity of my promise was such that nothing could relieve my pain.

One day Nina, who always had an idea or two about alleviating pain, said — so seriously that I almost didn't recognize her — "I know exactly the energy that you need."

I was skeptical but interested: "Is she blond and nice and loving and a nonneurotic fire sign?" I asked, pretty sure that such a combination did not exist.

"Yes," Nina said. "You can call Aetheria at this number if you want."

Nina was acting differently than ever before. When she mentioned Aetheria's name, an emanation of respect filled the room, and even Raz noticed the change. "Yes," he agreed, "Aetheria would be good for him. They are both so solemn."

I called Aetheria. "My name is Haiam," I said. "Nina gave me your name."

"Yes, she told me she was going to," replied Aetheria, and right away I too was filled with great respect. "What can I do for you?" she asked softly.

Her voice touched my heart, my arrogance moved aside, and I said very humbly, "May I come over?"

"Yes," she answered, and hung up.

After all the time I had spent in Oceana and all the girls I had seen, I figured I knew what would take place. I'd arrive, we'd go dancing and dining, and then we'd go to bed. Afterwards I'd see her a few times more, then get bored again. Maybe I shouldn't go, I thought. Yet I knew I would go — what else was there to do?

She lived in the country. I arrived at a small cottage in the middle of the woods. It seemed to be standing in its own space. (I thought "etheric space," but I wasn't to use such words.) It was sunset; the space surrounding the front door was bathed in pink, purple and gold. Approaching the door, I quieted myself, and my inner vibration came present and alive.

Aetheria opened the door. Her face was golden, cherubic — deep blue eyes, reddish cheeks, and a smile denoting inner satisfaction and peace. The smile extended beyond her face, filling her whole home.

"Would you like to come in?" she asked, bringing me out of my meditation.

"Certainly, thank you, excuse me," I said clumsily, entering the house.

Chapter 6

Aetheria

In Aetheria's simple hut everything emanated peace — the walls, the shelves, the plain furniture. I had seen so much luxury in various places, yet this emptiness made those environments seem poor by comparison. Even in Oceana I had seen women wearing diamonds, gold and pearls who looked like corpses wearing jewels. But here it was all so different. The wealth of this presence was indescribable.

"Indescribable" I said. "I *want* this. What is it?"

"Knowledge," she smiled. And closing her eyes she projected a total experience of solemn peace.

"Give it to me," I requested.

"I can't. It is knowledge of the Word. You have to go to Mahatma."

"Ma — what?" I had never heard such a word before.

"*Maha* is big, *atma* is Soul."

Arrogantly I said, "I thought all souls are just souls and there is no hierarchy of souls." Instantly I regretted my statement and corrected myself. During my time in the desert as well as in Oceana, I had contaminated my gentleness with the habits of the environment.

"I apologize for my harshness," I said, "but I've gone through hard times."

"I know," she smiled, closing her eyes again. "That is why you were sent here."

"How do you know?" I asked in surprise. Now I imagined that she knew all and everything about me; this gave me a glimmer of hope, since I had felt isolated for so long.

"I don't," she replied. "But the Word does."

I approached her. "I want you," I said, embracing her in a full-body hug.

She received me right away, not only in my body, but more. She also relieved me of my aloneness. That night we had sex in body and soul, and I knew that the way the soul made love in the body was through sex. What a contrast to my many pointless sexual adventures in Oceana!

The vibration crossed all my fields, my heart was opened, and I trusted fully in life's gentleness.

Chapter 7

Mahatma

The next morning, and the mornings after that, I woke up next to Aetheria. We made love all the time, and my contact with her was the most healing I had yet experienced. But my thirst for what she called "the experience of the knowledge" was growing, and with it my admiration for her way of living. For example, with her nothing went to waste.

"Want some corn?" she offered during dinner one night.

"Yes, thank you." I replied.

"Don't forget to bury it when you are through. All that we use we give back to Tria Ra, and it becomes new fertilizer. That is why living in the big city is like a desert—nothing grows there besides allergies."

"Allergies?" I asked, surprised.

"Yes," she responded, "allergies to nature, to life, and to each other. People get no recognition for truth, only for what is in the checkbook or maybe sometimes in the head. But not for what's in the heart; that doesn't count. You know that, don't you?"

Did I? I had seen cities throughout all my lives and had never correlated allergies with closed-in living. I knew that city people were sicker, but I hadn't made the connection.

"I guess I didn't," I answered. "Tell me more."

"The heart," she said, placing her right hand on the center of her chest, "is like a radar that recognizes itself in others who are in tune with their own heart. You know," she added, "I'm not talking about the tick-tock heart. I'm talking about this." And she again put her hand on the center of her chest. As she talked, the radiation of tremendous peace filled me. I relaxed deeper and deeper into the feeling of love. Now, even though I was loving myself, and even though I loved her in a sensuous, physical, friendly and romantic way, and even though I could remember my love for my mother and father, for other women and for friends, this love—the love I was feeling now—was something else.

"You must see the Perfect Master," she said.

"Perfect Master?"

"Yes. The love you are feeling is for him. Whoever truly learns to love him learns how to love." She smiled, secure in the certainty of her love.

"Aetheria," I said, "I feel so good here. I am resting in this love. Why must I see anyone?"

"So that you can always rest in the world, no matter where you are."

She sounded so truthful and simple. I looked at all that I knew, from outer space backward to the earth and onward to Tria Ra, yet I couldn't find a word to describe my current feelings.

"Aetheria," I said, "I love you so much."

"I love you too," she responded. "And our love will even grow bigger after you go and see the Perfect Master."

Most of the people I had loved in my life had been so possessive of me that I felt imprisoned. But here was Aetheria, sending me away from her toward my greater growth. Even though I wanted to stay with her, I also knew I had to go in search of the Perfect Master.

I didn't see her for a few days, and my heart grew fonder. I missed the presence of her voluptuous body next to mine, the radiation of her almost-visible mind, and above all the full and plentiful nourishment that emanated from her heart all the time, whether she was going out to work, burying some "organic garbage," or making love more passionately than anyone I had ever known. She was so fully in love, so present with everything she did that I found it hard to let go.

As the days went by I felt more and more attached to her.

One day she said, "My love, when you have knowledge you will love in a detached way."

"Who wants that?" I asked. I felt that nonattachment had been my way throughout my life, and that my greatest blessing was to find her resonant company.

"Your heart," she answered placidly. "Your heart wants to love freely. Then you can serve everyone. If you have no servant, then there is no service. And if there is no service, then there is no humility; and if there is no humility, then there is no human being."

I had arrogant thoughts: What did this girl know about Being? I had been Being for eternity, and knew it.

"That's exactly the way **not** *to use your own knowledge,"* interrupted the voice of the Master. *"That is why you are in School."*

In the midst of my romance I had forgotten that I was also in the midst of a new lesson. My enjoyment of the love had anesthetized my memories of purpose. I apologized, forgiving myself for my arrogance just as I heard Aetheria say, "After you see the Perfect Master, you won't forget the purpose of a human being's life."

"Hey, how did you know I was thinking of purpose?" I asked, expecting some esoteric response.

Instead she responded with a smile. I rushed toward her and we embraced in loving tenderness. With Aetheria, tenderness always moved on to passion, and the soul made love to the body each time our chemistries came close. After orgasm, all began again. It was like leaving our bodies, embracing our souls, and falling asleep into the mating of oneness for hours and hours of time — almost simply being a breath of life. This healing of past wounds or open sores in the emotional or mental bodies was creating a container to enclose my search for knowledge.

At last the news came to Oceana that Mahatma would come

to a place only twelve hours' drive away to show us the inner Perfect Master.

I arranged for my departure, thanking everyone I knew. Raz asked me to come back and let him know what happened. Aetheria promised to wait for me.

I joined a caravan of seekers in a van.

"Move over, this isn't a first-class airplane!" a young man exclaimed aggressively, pushing me with his guitar.

"Shut up!" said someone else, clipping his nails and spitting out the window.

"Listen," said the driver, "we'll have to behave like friendly brothers and sisters in search of the Truth. If not, I'll kick you off this van, which is *my* van. This includes you, too!" he told his fearful wife.

"Okay," I said, "as long as we get there on time."

"If we don't, then it wasn't meant to be," he replied defiantly. "In any case, if you want to go somewhere else, I'll let you off. Remember, I'm doing you a favor. You didn't even pay for gas."

Oh my, I thought. I hope we all get there alive.

The level of hostility grew as days of driving went by. "Fuck you all," said a girl in the back of the van, who had been silent for the whole journey. "I don't need any spiritual knowledge. I want dope."

"There's no dope in the van," said the driver, "but we can stop. I sure could use some."

So we did.

"Not for me," I said. "I'm waiting for initiation." This was met with grunts, jeers and stares, but later on some respected me for keeping my word.

Night was sometimes a relaxing change from the fumes and toxins of the van.

We stayed at several communities of the Perfect Master. The citizens were beautiful, open, gracious human beings. It was as if Aetheria had cloned herself in all of them. Their feeling for their Master was reflected in the way they said hello, shook hands, gave their food, lent their homes and were in harmony with themselves. I could see their beautiful Souls in their eyes as they shared with us their experience of their Selves.

Then we climbed back in the van again, where the contrast of grossness, inhumanity, violence and abuse was immediately exposed in every way. Alternating between bliss and nausea, I decided to call this preparation an exposure of cleansing in order to receive the Perfect Master in my heart.

"How do you know the Perfect Master is the One?" asked the Mahatma.

"I don't," I said.

"If you don't know it's he, then I can't initiate you into the knowledge of the Perfect One."

"But how could I know?" I asked.

"By experiencing the meditation that he gives."

"So initiate me."

"I can't if you don't know it's he."

This was evidently a Catch-22 situation. The experience of the knowledge was definitely something outside my realm of understanding.

I followed the Mahatma from hour to hour, arguing, discussing, impugning, trying to find out. His answer was only the constancy of his peaceful smile.

One day he said, "The only way in is to surrender."

"As in a war," I said.

"No, that is submission. Surrender, as in Love."

I remembered my surrender in the form of my relationship with Aetheria, that which she called attachment. I asked the Mahatma if it was the same.

He replied, "No, that is exactly what I was saying about submission. Surrender is like true Love in knowing who we truly are."

I flashed back to my youth and remembered Amada's song:

> Freedom is surrender
> and this surrender is Love.

Love that always Was
Love that always Is
Love that will always Be.
True Love is to remember
that which I truly Am.
Where hope deceives, there truths die,
Keeping only *promises* of Life forever.

"Yes, exactly," said the Mahatma. "That is it, the domain in which you become ready for initiation."

I wondered if Amada knew.

Chapter 8

The Perfect Master

Light, sound, fragrance, taste, nectar and, above all, the holy Word were the quintessential faculties awakened in me by the process of initiation.

The whole contingent from the van was transformed at the same time. When we looked at each other, we saw lightness, freshness, youth, smiles and a loving, respectful caring for each other.

"Now we are really brothers and sisters," said the driver.

"It was all worth it," we all said as one body.

Being one in the Spirit was meaningful, but being one with the community was even greater.

The secret process of initiation was so personal that it became sacred. I had rekindled the light of my Soul with Love, and a golden thread invisibly connected me like a flower in a garland to the heart of the Perfect Master.

He was always present in my heart, and my longing to be with him physically grew and grew.

~ ❧ ~

I went back to Oceana, and my friends did not recognize me. They thought I was so light that maybe I had died. Some accused me of being brainwashed, others of having been born again. Only Aetheria understood.

I told her, "I will see you again at the feet of the Perfect Master."

"I love you and respect your choice," she replied. "Know

that I am always here for you, and I know you must go now and follow your own path of Devotion."

Devotion, that was what it was. Devotion—the sweetest experience I had ever dreamed of. Brighter than the light of the sun, sweeter than the nectar of a thousand flowers, warmer than the shelter of fire, cooler than the breeze of the ocean, and fonder and closer to the heart than my own life.

As I stepped onto the airplane that would take me away from Oceana, I told Aetheria, "At the feet of the Master, you can really let it go, let it flow. We are all Love, Love, Love."

~ ❧ ~

North of Oceana I encountered thousands of people from all races of the world and all walks of life assembled in an open field, singing, chanting, dancing and looking into each other with peaceful eyes. All were immersed in the loving harmony of the spring sun and the green pastures, the open-ocean feeling of the lavender scent of flowers. But it was, above all, the experience of meditation deeply connecting our hearts that enabled us all to be free from personal or societal attachments and to experience the free flow of being alive. In such a state of well-being, I could enjoy the peace that now prevailed throughout my consciousness.

I was excited about meeting with the Perfect Master, but I was even more excited by the joyful, contented harmony that emanated from the depths of this community. How different from my previous autonomous way of living was this possibility of merging with a "higher source" of energy! Knowing that I was no longer alone allowed me to feel an even greater power than before.

"Aren't we fortunate to have been sewn into a garland of flowers to ornament the Perfect Master?" an Eastern Mahatma cried.

"Yes indeed," I reflected. There was such a peace in my heart that right now nothing could shatter it. There was no new information or high experience. There was only the encounter with the beloved Author; and soon I would encounter the Being whom most people around here called the embodiment of the

Lord. Whether or not this was true, I had never felt so united to the human race, and I wished all of humanity could have partaken of the feast.

The Festival of Light came to its highlight when the Master appeared. He was beautiful, young, strong, loving and very, very simple. "I am the source of Peace," he said, "and I can give it to you."

Thousands praised him, and as I looked from the observer role something shifted in my Self and I became a living part of the human body assembled here.

I knew that I wanted to serve, but I didn't know how. This was what I felt:

Ascended Life

The energies of Love
intoxicate
and swamp this soul of mine
into the realms
    where neither time
    nor thoughts
    nor thyme exist;
only the divine smile
prevails.

Oh wonderful, ecstatic song,
your grace brings forward
all that
which is its Essence —
is it mine?

I Am.

I Am the knower and the known:
prevailing strength,
amazing tune,
Beloved Source.

Rejoice!

The Lord within the heart
    has won
and all the shadows

sent away.
The trumpets play,
the end of time
has come.

A glorious sun
now shines
and in the center of this throne
Beloved Radiance
springs out
and claims

"It's mine,
that which thou
hath called the world.

"It's mine,
that which thou
hath called the flesh."
And for the third time
it shouts out,

"It's mine, that which thou
hath called the mind.

"I am the Lord
the King of time
the joyous One
behind the heart

"The one who travels
from the Source
Beyond matter
time
or
space."

Now I hear and express
that which is,
I listen and obey.
All of life continual
song must be,
And all expressions of this
breath.

The whip of life
the dance of soul must be.
So live in constant
harmony,
just be — tune in and
to your own self be true.

Set according to the heart
time by time and
step by step.
Be now, be here
Act now, act here.
Enjoy the musical act
of God —
in love
in peace
in that
which He enjoys:

Perfect Harmony.

Inflamed with the purpose to not dilute aliveness with mediocrity, I moved to a communal house and lived happily for some time in what was called an ashram.

I had many occasions to see the Master, but more and more his presence permeated every cell of my body, even in his physical absence. My devotion increased and culminated in a dedication to service. The more I served, the better my sense of purpose took hold in my Being.

The meditations and spiritual lectures were simple and pure, but constantly full of inspiration to go deeper into the Heart, to love my Self and to share this love with my fellow beings.

Becoming a lover in this way was the most rewarding phase of my life. Nothing made any sense without it. Devotion is the purpose of human life, and any action done in the consciousness of love was Love itself.

Years went by, and the rhythm of living, serving and loving

was uniting my sense of being in the human body. I no longer saw the body as a vehicle — it was more like the embodiment of Love in matter. Love — that precious chemical force that enables us to give and work and Be. Blessed was the Master's form. Thanks to him, I was fast transcending all separation from the physical and spiritual domain.

My usual way of thinking was confronted. When the alter ego was confronted with the greatness of pure Love, it reacted by introducing images to counteract the truth. And yet at this stage I lived a life of balance — for each outer act, an inner awareness was performed; for each external sight, there was inner sight with the knowledge of divine Light; for each sound, there was the inner aspect of the harmony of the Soul; for each outer expression, there was the self-expression of the Word resonating inside the Self; and for each flavor/taste there was the taste of Grace, the impalpable but real quality that was keeping all in place.

It was a marvelous time of great concentration upon perfection within my Self.

Chapter 9

Into the World

"What do you think you have been doing?" asked the Cat early one morning, interrupting my dreams at a time when I usually was getting up for meditation.

"Hi!" I said. For a long time its presence, as well as the qualities of Essence, had been in the background of my consciousness. "I've been fine," I said, "and I wish to continue in this ashram for the rest of my life." I had taken the vows of poverty, chastity and obedience; I seemed to be rejuvenating day by day.

"That's very nice," injected the Cat, *"but would it now be time to share?"*

"I *am* sharing—with my brothers and sisters. We live in a very harmonious communal life and praise Love and Life in all of our actions."

"I will arrange a circumstance for you," said the voice.

"Aha!" I said. "Again there is a shift in the teaching!"

"Yes," answered the voice. *"I will arrange a circumstance in which you will be tested. Seven years of refuge is fine. Now it's time to spend some time in the world and to test yourself in giving."*

"But that's all I *have* been doing," I said, noticing how much attachment I had developed for this way of life.

"Giving, yes—but how about business?" asked the Cat. *"Can you support yourself while supporting others? Can you integrate your heart in your profession in a more than typical, traditional way?"*

"It's time to go into the world," added Augustus. *"We will create a circumstance so you can go home. And then you'll stay and work."*

"Home?" I said in surprise. "*This* is home. I've surrendered to the Perfect Master."

"Good," added the golden sapphire of Certainty. *"Then you are at one with him."*

"Well," I said, "I don't know that."

"You will," Androgynous affirmed, shining his green emerald in my eyes. *"You will."*

The words of the qualities of Essence seemed cold to me. All I really wanted was to stay in the ashram for the rest of my life. Little did I know what Beauty had prepared for me.

At a spiritual festival in a neighboring city, I ended up sitting next to a simple woman, from whom all qualities of beauty beamed. Without knowing what was happening, I found myself renouncing renunciation and going on the road with her. It never was pleasant, but lust and passion's image invaded my awareness, and soon I was earning a living to support us. As soon as I was established, she left my life — and my memory — as fast as she had entered.

Now I needed to share with my own people what it meant to feel so good within myself after a year of working hard and learning the perils of transactions in a world that valued currencies more than life itself. I found myself at home, visiting my parents.

"Haiam is here!" cried my sister breathlessly. "Haiam!"

"So many years! We thought we'd never see you again," wept Lakshmi, embracing me.

Even Arcanus shed some tears.

"It's wonderful to have you here," said Amada, who by this time was happily married and had three children.

I played with them, I was one of them, and I learned of my ability to fully communicate with babies.

"Now you will settle down and give us some grandchildren, and we will be the family of love we always were," my parents urged.

Family of Love — how do they know the name of my community? I thought. Maybe *this* is what I needed to learn.

"Again, you have an option," said the voice. *"Bring the love you've learned into the comfort of your family home, or make yourself separate."*

"Will the lessons ever end?"

"Yes," answered the voice harshly, *"when you do!"*

I had to stay and look at all the reactions. This was my growing up. The connection I had built to my home had to be confronted; I saw come up again and again the dodecagram of ego traits, which had been generated by the corrupting demon of negative love and reaffirmed by the lack of knowledge of the Self. Each person wanted me to be according to their way. I could only be the way I was.

I learned how to breathe from a deeper center within myself. One day as I was sitting in my room (the room in which my body grew up), I saw stardust fall on me. As it took a shape, Forgiveness came forward, and I said, guided by its Essence: "I forgive myself and accept myself for being as I am. I have surrendered to Love and cannot serve two gods at the same time. The god of opinions must now die."

I shook all over, burst into tears and left my body in my astral coat as I had not done in a very long time. Thus I connected with Lakshmi and said, "I forgive you for being how you are, and for everything I learned from you I thank you and praise our God." As I cleared the blame and guilt, the left side of my body came alive and totally present; when I also forgave and thanked Arcanus, the right side of my body came alive and fully present. I was free.

"I am free!" I said laughing, rushing down the stairs. "I understand how we share, what we have, and how it relates to what we do in life!"

My parents were astonished at my strange reaction, but they too felt a release.

Curiously enough, with my presence in the house their health improved.

Tria Ra was in the final stage of suppression. The warlords so limited the food supplies — physical food, emotional food, mental food — that there hardly was any nourishment in people's interactions. Death was considered a final phenomenon, and many people wished that it would come soon.

There was so much hunger for spiritual food that people believed in leadership that came from the show business/pornographic worlds, and the hope of survival sustained everybody.

Communities based on Light and Love were outlawed, and other esoteric teachings were ridiculed. The Masters were in jails, in which people were exhibited as in zoos.

"Survival of the fittest" was the law of the land, just like on earth in its latter days. As I became aware of the situation, I thought, I don't really know what to do except to speak the truth. But if I do, I might end up in jail.

"What do you want?" asked the Cat. Over the past months, he had become a close presence again.

I said, "I want to serve. I want that which every Soul on earth wants and doesn't know how to express."

"Make a movie of the Teaching," advised the Cat. *"It would affect great numbers of people, who might change their minds and choose to seek Life."*

"Write a book," said Augustus. *"It will remain forever."*

This was the first time I saw any disagreement within my inner court. The overpowering energies of current reality in Tria Ra were present.

So I aligned my body and called on my angels to mediate. As I was in the Light, enjoying the pure Word and delighting in divine nectar, the prayer in my heart went on and on. It was like the prayer of St. Francis, but modified:

I Am, Lord of the Universe

Make me an instrument of your peace:
Where there is darkness, let my essence of Universal
Consciousness shine Your Light.
Where there is sorrow, make me a reason for your Joy.
Where there is hunger, let me feed the poor.

Where there is sickness, let health shine forth.
Let me use this life of Ours
Not to be a grain of sand, which is harsh and solid,
But let me become a drop of honey
Which, in its sweetness, can heal;
Which, in its fluidity, can flow with the course of time;
Which, with its golden absorbed Light, can speak to the
Wholeness of
I Am, Lord of the Universe.
Let our glory now prevail so that on the material plane
Only Love and Learning will
Proclaim
The Glory of Oneness in the Universe,
Divine Principle which integrates body, Spirit, man and
science in the Wholeness of
I Am, Lord of the Universe.

"That's it!" I said. "I want to serve and be consumed, to be used up to the fullest. As a candle shines to its last moment, so am I committed to the Work."

"Remember now," said the Cat, *"how important it is not to become a specialist but to integrate the tuning of the physical instrument."*

And as suddenly as if I'd been hit by a ray of light, the promise not to use my powers was lifted.

Chapter 10

Time to Teach

The word traveled fast in this city. "How did you know I was here?" I asked Luciane, my friend and companion from medical school.

"I felt you," she answered, "and you are here at the perfect time. I'm in trouble, and I feel you can help me."

My first assignment was on. *"Keep humble,"* said Augustus, *"because what you are about to do is utterly new for you — at least in the last few lifetimes."*

Luciane's mother was in a coma and was dying. Intuitively, I knew that within three days she would leave her body forever. And Luciane had not completed her relationship with her.

As hard as it is to be attached to another soul when they are in the body, still there is a chance to overcome distance and to clear the bond. But when someone died on Tria Ra, the survivors believed that life was ended forever; so they carried the burden of their passion, which usually was confined to sadness, remorse or guilt, for as long as they carried a body.

So I was being asked to mediate in what is called a life/death event. Throughout the material plane, people's major inner concerns had to do with life and death.

It was around this subject — the perishability of the body — that human beings would come to terms with themselves and their relatives. Certainly, the fear of incompleteness that Luciane was experiencing, now that her mother was in a coma, caused her not only to open up her natural perceptions (which enabled her to recognize my presence in town, after so many years of absence) but also to penetrate her pride (which enabled her to request my assistance). As for me, I opened myself up totally to the possibility of service.

I was full of joy about being able to serve and full of uncertainty about what form this would require.

Little did I know that this death experience would open up the path to a new dimension — one of unconditional service regardless of circumstance — and teach me about the energy involved in human groups.

As I entered the clinic in which Luciane's mother was dying, I could see the fear in my friend. It was common to wait to the last moment before acknowledging gratitude for the dying person's service, and so did Luciane. I told her to create, with full certainty, the intention to communicate; and right there in front of my very eyes Luciane's mother came out of her coma and completed her relationship with her daughter. As they both embraced, letting go of attachments, Love filled the room and the old woman died.

Luciane looked at me. "Thank you," she said, completely in balance. "Thank you very much."

I had been meditating on the Holy Name, the inner Word, throughout the whole experience. "I am at peace, so is your mother and so are you," I said. "God bless you all." I had been the mediator of one of the most solemn transitions a human being can have: leaving the physical domain.

Nowhere had we learned in medical school to forgive each other and thus ease transitions. Death was to be avoided, and thus the completion of the life cycle was always disregarded.

"The journey of a soul is such," I told Luciane, "that it needs balance at all times. We focus on the birth, but we forget the death. Even the word 'death' has a charge that tends to scare people off."

"Why is that?" she asked.

"Because in that way the forces of Imago control us and have us do the physical labors. They want to feed its needs."

"Imago?" she said. "What's that?"

"The Imago forms that we feel, project and make believe are real. It's like fashions that monitor our behaviors and then enslave our lives. Thus we live at the effect of circumstances and try to create new circumstances to change the old ones. That is how negative emotions arise that bind humans into the enslavement of relations such as the one you now have cleared." All this I asserted with a strength I had never before experienced.

"Fascinating," said the new orphan. "I'd like to hear more about it. Can you come for tea?"

"Indeed," I agreed.

At her house there was little talk, only condolences and mourning rites. Throughout, Luciane kept looking at me and winking to acknowledge our secret complicity.

As she watched me, I sat vibrating the soul of Peace.

In the background I heard some of the mourners asking, "Who is that man? He seems to be at peace."

~ ❧ ~

Peace, I thought, is a relative condition — especially in a world where change constantly prevails. Not knowing what the next step in my life would be, I invoked the presence of my Council of Twelve.

"It looks like it is time to manifest," said William. *"All these people here could use your skill for better living."*

"The strength that you have must be put into service," said the Cat.

"I must have a channel through which to express myself," added both Androgynous and Augustus.

And so each one went on, presenting his or her own case.

Meditating, I only saw the balance in my Self.

"Indeed," said the voice, *"peace is a relative condition that can expand as it shares itself."*

"Yes," I agreed, "I know that I must share. But what's the proper vehicle for doing it?"

"Your Self," the Cat said bluntly.

This was of no help. But — as it is common in life — an opportunity arose that enabled me to change the whole course of my life for the next seven years. Luciane asked whether I would be willing to perform the ceremony at her mother's funeral.

"Funeral?" I asked in surprise. "I've never done anything like this before."

"You were the closest to us toward the end," she insisted. "No one else has the authority to say a thing."

"All right," I agreed, "but I don't know what to say."

At the funeral I did know. I don't quite remember what it was I said, but I do remember that the faces of the attendants lightened up and that a traditionally sad event became a celebration of rebirth.

When I spoke of the "leaving of a Soul" instead of the "dying of a body," everyone rejoiced. And it was this inspiration that caused the shift in my life.

"Teach us what you know," said a young professional. "Get a group together and we shall work on transformation."

Transformation? "Yes," I answered. The capacity to unfold from a cocoon to a butterfly.

~ ❧ ~

Over the next few months the consciousness of Tria Ra's people opened, and wherever I went masses of people were transforming — growing, learning, living, loving and above all, unfolding into the beauty of themselves.

The cycle had finally been reversed. The forces of Light were enabling us to create channels and networks of communication in which telepathic abilities were the common way to relate.

"This is the time for completion," said Amada joyously, watching our own father, Arcanus, clear his karmic record and become the essential Being we always knew he was.

A funeral had sponsored a rebirth not only for me but for many friends in the human race.

I was working with full expenditure of my energy for long periods of time. My vitality was strong, and I believed that the New Age had just begun for all.

"Not so fast," said the Cat. *"In this time of completion, something else will happen."*

"What's that?" I asked, surprised at his seriousness.

"Completion creates a space for everything that is incomplete, for each karmic form to express itself until it completes itself."

"How is that?"

"Whatever was ever begun and not fulfilled is inscribed in the cosmic memory of each one on Tria Ra," said Augustus. *"All thoughts, feelings, actions, words and deeds that still have electric charge around them – that is, that are activated – need to neutralize, whether the charge is in the physical body or any other impression on the Soul."*

"Is that what they call karma?" I asked.

"Yes, karma is what indicates where energy is stuck – records that need to be cleared and filed away."

"Oh God," I said, "then heavy times are coming through this opening of Light."

"Indeed," said Androgynous. *"It is like entering a dark room: When it's fully dark, you don't see the dirt. At first, when light enters, you rejoice; but then there is no more excuse not to go in and clean the dirt up."*

"And," Augustus concluded, *"you get to see all that unfinished business, and you get the opportunity to clean it up. This creates Wisdom."*

"So with transformation, we created a bigger mess to clean up than was here before?" I asked tentatively.

"Enlightenment can't live where darkness prevails. Infinity can't be where finiteness reigns. One of the two has to go – and usually it's not infinity," said the Cat, mocking my fear. *"This fear is the last veil you need to cross. When you see it as illusion, you become free. But it isn't easy."*

Meanwhile, more and more people were attracted to the teachings that came forward through me.

"It's so beautiful to see them bloom and grow and create lives of their own," said my Authenticity.

"What about me?" I asked Luciane, who had become my

main assistant. "I feel like just a channel through which all this flows."

"You need to find your own love," she said, seeing me consumed by the work. "Everyone needs a Soulmate to share the energies of life. And maybe that will be your own completion, since it seems to me that by yourself you are whole."

~ ❧ ~

The condition of Tria Ra was inflamed.

More and more, weaponry, propaganda, separation of human values according to permitted standards, and adoration of currency by the leaders were creating conditions of separation in portions of the planet. It reminded me of the Age of Pagan on earth. An epilogue?

But this time there was a difference — this time completion was taking place for all; and throughout all the material planes, Soul-aware survivors on different material planets were working on the equivalents of transformative living. Transmutation was at hand.

This enabled the whole galaxy to start to elevate their own vibrational rate accordingly.

Thinking about the self-destruction of the physical did not threaten my faith, even though it did torture my memory many times a day.

As darkness demonstrated its powers by suppressing the right to think, speak and act, more and more people were learning to transcend the physical and to project their Essence to remote places outside of Tria Ra's orbit, therefore bathing the planet in their own Light beyond their grid.

Completion was an interesting phenomenon. Representatives of all cults, ideals, philosophies and religions were increasing throughout the planet, attracting people who, in external appearance, seemed to have nothing to do with those ideas but who needed to dramatize an old memory from other lives by adhering to that representative belief.

Relationships were short-lived. People would get married to complete old actions and then separate, moving on with the expansion of their lives. Earth divorces had been battles of animosity; Tria Ra divorces were accepted as workouts toward completion.

Children came into the material plane with adult diseases. Shortly afterward they died, never to incarnate again. Ascension was at hand.

Medical science was at a loss to understand the speed of these changes. Only the force of transformation helped people to comprehend the accelerated process of growth that we entered toward the end of Tria Ra's time.

"So much learning—and all this for another big completion," I said.

"And integration," added Augustus.

"Plus, there is still your work to be done," added the Cat. *"When your instrument is fully tuned..."*

"Not again!" I interrupted.

"...it will resonate with another one in such a way that you will have a child. Remember the starting of a New Race."

"But with whom," I asked, "and where?"

"This planet is about to blow up like earth did once. Maybe this time it will split in two and not blow up."

"In two?" I asked, unable to make sense of it.

"Yes," said Augustus, *"in two—one planet for the inhabitants of a higher frequency and one for those who still need to incarnate and work some things out."*

"Do not interpret this as good or bad," added the Cat. *"It's just different classes in the School."*

"All of you who have worked together will vibrate toward one planet; the others will go to the other," added Augustus.

Despite the knowledge, light, heart, love and beauty I had experienced, I also saw that I had things to work out for many years to come. It wasn't as if I were a pure Being. An aspect was materially inclined, and despite the work of transformation, there were alter egos at play.

I wondered where I was to go, still thinking of myself with a certain degree of doubt.

"That part definitely belongs in the material plane," said the Cat. *"To answer your doubts, maybe you should plan on tuning the physical instrument and meditate to attract your Soulmate.*

"Time," he said, while we listened to the news about the beginning of the psychotronic wars, *"is running short."*

Chapter 11

The Beginning

The psychotronic war was the cleanest means of violence I had ever seen throughout all the universe.

Using the discoveries of transmutation, belligerent forces were seizing each others' minds and bombarding each others' fields with particles, thus creating confusion in their antagonists' minds and destabilizing the molecules in their bodies and either paralyzing them or stopping them from functioning clearly.

Meanwhile, Tria Ra's air became so solid that we could walk in space. A new industry, space cars, was flourishing. It was easy to drive out of the planetary system, but it was also very risky: The psychotronic particles could crystallize one's body in space. The network of conscious communion throughout the universe was constantly emitting Light to neutralize the fields, but the forces of darkness seemed to be in control. It looked like the comedy was going to play itself out to completion.

I spent most of my days deeply absorbed in I Am.

One morning I saw a billboard ad that read: "Perfect Union: Attraction of Your Mate—A Seminar for Enlightened Souls." This seemed so attractive to me that I went to the address indicated.

And there she was. Bhakti-Shadai, whom I had not seen since my medical school years. We looked at one another and embraced. But Soulmates were not who we were. Masters of Light we are. Ascended Masters had found each other to be the seeds of a new civilization.

This time the embrace produced a child, and then another

child. Children of Spirit. A boy and a girl. But truly Masters of Light.

~ ❧ ~

Eliyanand and Aeterne were born in perfect harmony – in the midst of splitting worlds.

The rest of the story we all know.

The etheric force rearranged the planet into two frequencies, each spinning at different frequencies. The mental-feeling-physical bodies remained on the lower-vibration planet, devoid of image and completing their life cycles through the distant guidance of those of us on the higher-vibration planet. They considered us Spirit Guides. Eventually that will be worked out: The absence of Imago allows for true guidance and Ascension. The prophecy fulfills itself.

~ ❧ ~

Aeterne and Eliyanand, this journey in this ship is not only to show you how it all was. It is also a surveillance trip to find out how the Mission is proceeding.

Those on the lower-frequency planet call us their Spirit Force, not knowing that they *are* us.

We are this new race, the race of the Beginning – Souls covered with the etheric robe, responsible for all the levels while all the other parts evolve into individuation.

Once again the universe is at peace.

So, my children, the bliss you are now experiencing wasn't always possible. Evolvement was needed to learn to appreciate what physical expression is all about. And thus this mutation took place.

"Observe well," I said to the children, while Bhakti-Shadai nursed Eliyanand.

Bhakti and I embraced. The Spirit had finally met.

"Thank you," said the children together.

"What did they say?" we asked each other.

Eliyanand repeated his very first spoken word: "Thank you."

Now it's time to go back home. To be at Source where gratitude and generosity prevail.

~ ❧ ~

Thus the prophecy was fulfilled. I whispered to Aeterna; Eliyanand smiled. The gentle separation of Tria Ra was completed. The doorway for everlasting joy was opened by the Grace of the true Christ as Divine Consciousness opened its arms and showered its Spirit on me. With that, Universal Consciousness entered the planetary grids. I felt that my nervous system had transmuted itself into new gold-copper wiring. It seemed to me that the baptism of fire had to follow the cleansing of water, for in the ancient Egyptian initiations on earth, the physical body was transmuted into a fifth-dimensional golden body. This was exerienced by all pharoahs when crowned with the symbolic Upper and Lower Kingdoms and is also experienced by Souls as they remember.

In this multidimensional space the children smiled and agreed whole-spiritedly on the perfection of cycles, which decode and translate genetic planetary memories into the cosmic Oneness. This was the time of a new beginning. We all remembered from our Essence the presence of Archangel Michael. He had been the witness of all cycles and the guardian of the wearing of the celestial robes in the corridor between dimensions.

The dark legends of Imago that had been left behind on the electromagnetic force fields of the frontiers of the lower dimensions had allowed the breath to be conferred upon man, transforming him to hu-man. Thus were the lessons to be mastered surpassed — lessons of not only the citizens of Tria Ra and earth/Terra but of all parallel planets once and forever into Ascension.

About the Author

Where can we look for living models and true direction to do the inner work needed to establish ourselves in the essence of our real identity?

Dr. Warter has journeyed from the world of traditional medicine and psychiatry to experiential insights derived from the teachings of the sacred traditions, returning to ordinary life to practice psychosynergy, a grounded and integrated approach to practical spirituality. He has coined the term psychosynergy —synergy of the mind and soul—for his unique synthesis of ancient knowledge and personal essence within the context of contemporary psychological and spiritual teaching.

Chilean born, Warter is the founder of the World Health Foundation for Development and Peace, and Heartnet International, and was awarded the United Nations Peace Messenger Award in 1987. He has served as a keynote speaker at Unity churches, medical and scientific associations, and business and consciousness gatherings around the world. Dr. Warter has authored a dozen books, published in Spanish, Romanian and English; his first essay was prefaced by Pablo Neruda, a Chilean mystic, poet and politician who was awarded the Nobel Prize in Literature in 1973 and a source of personal inspiration and guidance. Warter's work with Sufi teachers of different orders was a major influence for his latest book, *Recovery of the Sacred: Lessons in Soul Awareness* (HCI, 1995).

Through Heartnet International he conducts retreats and seminars in his hometown (Sedona, Arizona) as well as in sacred sites in Peru, Anatolia and Europe, and his work in psychosynergy is available in books, audio/video productions and personal group work. He is available for lecturing, consultation and academic mentoring through the facilities of the International University of Professional Studies.

Dr. Warter encourages readers' response to this work and how it assists their growth process.

Heartnet International
8776 E. Shea Blvd., B-3A-429
Scottsdale, AZ 85260
e mail: heartnet@aol.com

BOOK MARKET

A reader's guide to the extraordinary books we publish, print and market for your enLightenment.

ORDER NOW!
1-800-450-0985
or Fax 1-800-393-7017
Or use order form at end

VISA MasterCard

NEW!
THE EXPLORER RACE
Robert Shapiro/Zoosh

In this expansive overview, Zoosh explains, "You are the Explorer Race. Learn about your journey before coming to this Earth, your evolution here and what lies ahead." Topics range from ETs and UFOs to relationships.

$25.00 Softcover 650p ISBN 0-929385-38-1

NEW!
ETs AND THE EXPLORER RACE
Robert Shapiro/Joopah

The next book in the famous Explorer Race series. Covers the Grays, abductions, the genetic experiment, UFO encounters, contactees, the future of our relationship with various ETs and much more.

$14.95 softcover ISBN 0-929385-79-9

BEHOLD A PALE HORSE
William Cooper

Former U.S. Naval Intelligence Briefing Team Member reveals information kept secret by our government since the 1940s. UFOs, the J.F.K. assassination, the Secret Government, the war on drugs and more by the world's leading expert on UFOs.

$25.00 Softcover 500p ISBN 0-929385-22-5

✦ BOOKS BY LIGHT TECHNOLOGY RESEARCH

SHINING THE LIGHT

Revelations about the Secret Government and their connections with ETs. Information about renegade ETs mining the Moon, ancient Pleiadian warships, underground alien bases and many more startling facts.

SHINING THE LIGHT
BOOK II

Continuing the story of the Secret Government and alien involvement. Also information about the Photon Belt, cosmic holograms photographed in the sky, a new vortex forming near Sedona, and nefarious mining on sacred Hopi land.

SHINING THE LIGHT
BOOK III

The focus shifts from the dastardly deeds of the Secret Government to humanity's role in creation. The Earth receives unprecedented aid from Creator and cosmic councils, who recently lifted us beyond the third dimension to avert a great catastrophe.

VORTEX GUIDEBOOK
by 12 channels

200-plus pages of channeled, never-before-published information on the vortex energies of Sedona and the techniques to enable you to use the vortexes as multidimensional portals to time, space and other realities.

$14.95 Softcover 236p ISBN 0-929385-25-X

THE ALIEN PRESENCE
Evidence of secret government contact with alien life forms.
Ananda

Documented testimony of the cover-up from a U.S. president's meeting to the tactics of suppression. The most complete information yet available.

$19.95 Softcover ISBN 0-929385-64-0

MEDICINE
The Secrets of Color Vibrational Healing
Charles Klotsche

A practitioner's manual for restoring blocked energy to the body systems with specific color wavelengths by the founder of "The 49th Vibrational Technique."

$11.95 Softcover 114p ISBN 0-929385-27-6

✦ BOOKS BY DOROTHY ROEDER

THE NEXT DIMENSION IS LOVE
Ranoash

As speaker for a civilization whose species is more advanced, the entity describes the help they offer humanity by clearing the DNA. An exciting vision of our possibilities and future.

$11.95 Softcover 148p ISBN 0-929385-50-0

REACH FOR US
Your Cosmic Teachers and Friends

Messages from Teachers, Ascended Masters and the Space Command explain the role they play in bringing the Divine Plan to the Earth now!

$14.95 Softcover 204p ISBN 0-929385-69-1

CRYSTAL CO-CREATORS

A fascinating exploration of 100 forms of crystals, describing specific uses and their purpose, from the spiritual to the cellular, as agents of change. It clarifies the role of crystals in our awakening.

$14.95 Softcover 288p ISBN 0-929385-40-3

BOOK MARKET

A reader's guide to the extraordinary books we publish, print and market for your enLightenment.

ORDER NOW!
1-800-450-0985
or Fax 1-800-393-7017
Or use order form at end

F THE ASCENSION BOOK SERIES by JOSHUA DAVID STONE, Ph.D.

THE COMPLETE ASCENSION MANUAL
How to Achieve Ascension in This Lifetime

A synthesis of the past and guidance for ascension. An extraordinary compendium of practical techniques and spiritual history. Compiled from research and channeled information.

$14.95 Softcover 297p ISBN 0-929385-55-1

SOUL PSYCHOLOGY
Keys to Ascension

Modern psychology deals exclusively with personality, ignoring the dimensions of spirit and soul. This book provides ground-breaking theories and techniques for healing and self-realization.

$14.95 Softcover 276p ISBN 0-929385-56-X

BEYOND ASCENSION
How to Complete the Seven Levels of Initiation

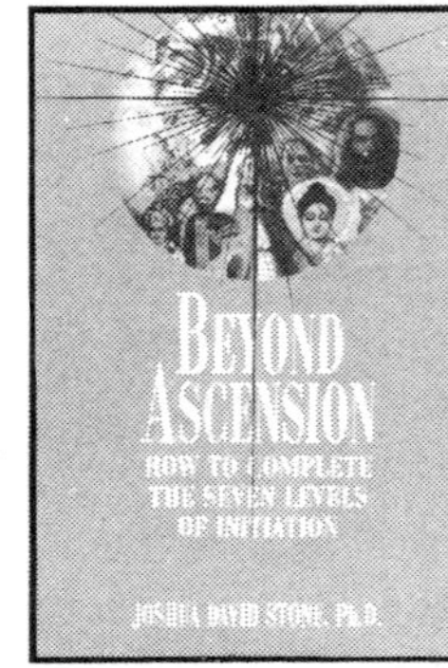

Brings forth new channeled material that demystifies the 7 levels of initiation and how to attain them. It contains new information on how to open and anchor our 36 chakras.

$14.95 Softcover 279p ISBN 0-929385-73-X

HIDDEN MYSTERIES
An Overview of History's Secrets from Mystery Schools to ET Contacts

Explores the unknown and suppressed aspects of Earth's past; reveals new information on the ET movement and secret teachings of the ancient Master

THE ASCENDED MASTERS LIGHT THE WAY
Keys to Spiritual Mastery from Those Who Achieved It

Lives and teachings of 40 of the world's greatest saints and spiritual beacons provide a blueprint for total self-realization. Guidance from those who mastered the secrets in their life-

ASCENSION-ACTIVATION TAPES

How to anchor and open your 36 chakras and build your light quotient at a speed never dreamed possible. Scores of new ascension techniques and meditations directly from the galactic and universal core.

ASCENSION-ACTIVATION MEDITATION TAPE:

- S101
- S102
- S103
- S104
- S105

$12.00 each

TECHNIQUES
That Trigger Transformation

Expanding the Heart Center . . . Launching your Light . . . Releasing the destructive focus . . . Weaving a Garment of Light . . . Light Alignment & more. A wonderfully effective tool for using Light to transcend. Beautiful guidance!

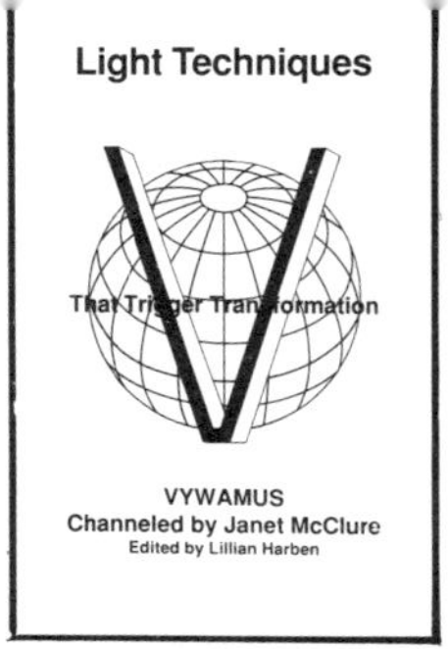

$11.95 Softcover 145p
ISBN 0-929385-00-4

ADVENTURE

Life is discovery, and this book is a journey of discovery "to learn, to grow, to recognize the opportunities – to be aware." It asks the big question, "Why are you here?" and leads the reader to examine the most significant questions of a lifetime.

$11.95 Softcover 157p
ISBN 0-929385-06-3

DIMENSIONS

Vywamus explains the process of exploring and experiencing the dimensions. He teaches an integrated way to utilize the combined strengths of each dimension. It is a how-to guidebook for living in the multi-dimensional reality that is our true evolutionary path.

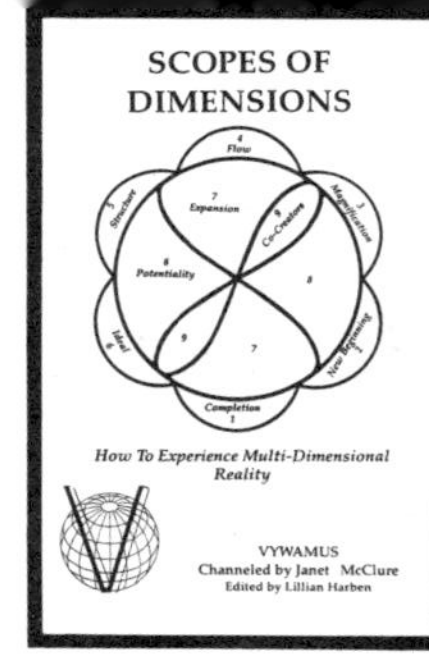

$11.95 Softcover 176p
ISBN 0-929385-09-8

AHA! The Realization Book
w/ Lillian Harben

If you are mirroring your life in a way that is not desirable, this book can help you locate murky areas and make them "suddenly . . . crystal clear." Readers will find it an exciting step-by-step path to changing and evolving lives.

$11.95 Softcover 120p
ISBN 0-929385-14-4

SANAT KUMARA
Training a Planetary Logos

How was the beauty of this world created? The answer is in the story of Earth's Logos, the great being Sanat Kumara. A journey through his eyes as he learns the real-life lessons of training along the path of mastery.

$11.95 Softcover 179p
ISBN 0-929385-17-9

NEW!
COCREATOR UNIVERSITY
Vywamus, Djwhal Khul & Atlanto

Your four bodies, the Tibetan Lesson series, the Twelve Rays, the Cosmic Walk-in and others. All previously unpublished channelings by Janet McClure.

$14.95 Softcover
ISBN 0-929385-54-3

BOOK MARKET

A reader's guide to the extraordinary books we publish, print and market for your enLightenment.

ORDER NOW!
1-800-450-0985
or Fax 1-800-393-7017
Or use order form at end

✦ BOOK AND MEDITATION TAPES by VYWAMUS/BARBARA BURNS

CHANNELLING:
Evolutionary Exercises for Channels

A lucid, step-by-step guide for experienced or aspiring channels. Opens the self to Source with simple yet effective exercises. Barbara has worked with Vywamus since 1987.

$9.95 Softcover 118p ISBN 0-929385-35-7

THE QUANTUM MECHANICAL YOU
Workshop presented by the *Sedona Journal of Emergence!* in Sedona April 2-3, 1994

Barbara Burns channeling through Vywamus explores the "mutational" process that humanity agreed to undertake at the time of the Harmonic Convergence.

This fundamental biochemical and electromagnetic restructuring is necessary for those who have agreed to remain in body throughout the full shift. The "mutation" process is a complete reformatting of the human DNA.

The workshop assisted understanding what is transforming in the body from both a microcosmic and macrocosmic perspective. Practical applications of exercises facilitate the mutation of the DNA in a balanced manner.

B101-4 (6-tape set) **$40**

✦ BOOK AND MEDITATION TAPES by BRIAN GRATTAN

MAHATMA I & II
Brian Grattan

Combined version of the original two books. Guidance to reach an evolutionary level of integration for conscious ascension. Fascinating diagrams, meditations, conversations.

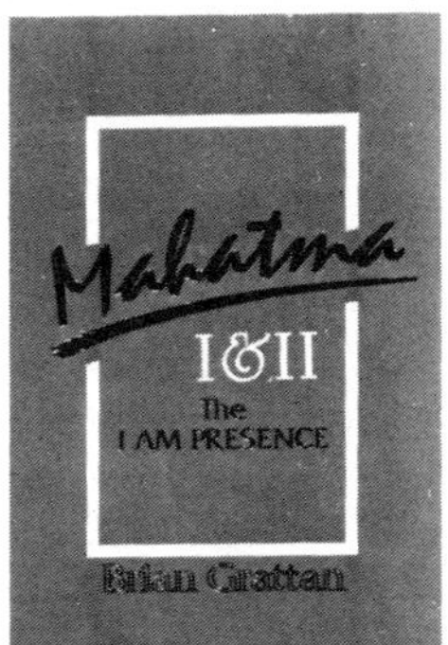

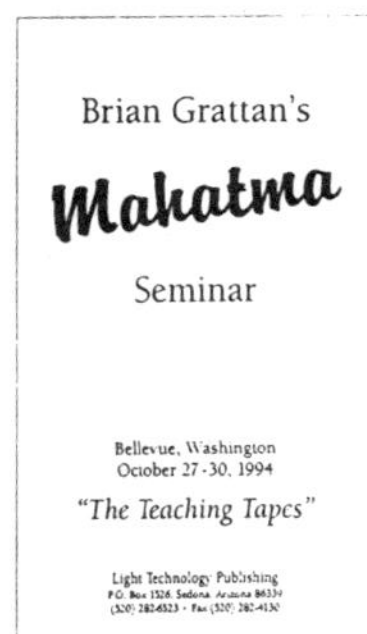

DNA FOR THE MULTIDIMENSIONAL MATRIX
Seattle Seminar, October 27-30, 1994

These 12 powerful tapes (which include 12 hours of meditations) lead to total spiritual transformation by recoding your 2-strand DNA to function in positive mutation, which finite scientists refer to as "junk" DNA.

Ancient intergalactic civilizations altered humanity so they would have to function with only 2% of their original 12 strands of DNA. The ultimate achievement now for Earth's inhabitants is to spiritualize the 12-strand DNA to achieve complete universal and monadic consciousness; these audio tapes are a profound step in that direction.

ON BECOMING

- Knowing the power of the light that you are
- Expansion of the pituitary gland and strengthening the physical structure
- Becoming more of you

F101 $10

HEALING MEDITATIONS/KNOWING SELF

- Knowing self is knowing God
- Knowing the pyramid of the soul is knowing the body
- Meditation to instruct you in the working of the soul and the use of the gold light within the body

F102 $10

MANIFESTATION & ALIGNMENT with the POLES

- This tape aligns your meridians with the grid system of the planet and connects the root chakra with the center of the planet.

F103 $10

THE ART OF SHUTTING UP

- Gaining the power and the wisdom of the quiet being that resides within the sight of thy Father.

F104 $10

CONTINUITY OF CONSCIOUSNESS

- Trains you in the powerful state of waking meditation.

F105 $25 (3-tape set)

BLACK-HOLE MEDITATION

- Personal mission; uniting with the Tribe.

F106 $10

MERGING THE GOLDEN LIGHT REPLICAS OF YOU

- Awakening to the master within your physical form.

F107 $10

NEW! SOULS, EVOLUTION AND THE FATHER

Channeling Lord God Jehovah

Lucifer's declaration begins the process of beings thinking another is greater than self. About the creation of souls; a way to get beyond doubt; how souls began to create physical bodies.

$12.95 Softcover 200p ISBN 0-929385-33-0

SIMON

A compilation of some of the experiences Arthur has had with the dolphins, which triggered his opening and awakening as a channel.

$9.95 Softcover 56p ISBN 0-929385-32-2

BOOK MARKET

A reader's guide to the extraordinary books we publish, print and market for your enLightenment.

ORDER NOW!
1-800-450-0985
or Fax 1-800-393-7017
Or use order form at end

VISA MasterCard

✦ BOOKS by HALLIE DEERING

LIGHT FROM THE ANGELS

Channeling the Angel Academy

Now those who cannot attend the Angel Academy in person can meet the Rose Angels who share their metaphysical wisdom and technology in this fascinating book.

$15.00 Softcover 230p ISBN 0-929385-72-1

DO-IT-YOURSELF POWER TOOLS

Assemble your own glass disks that holographically amplify energy to heal trauma, open the heart & mind, destroy negative thought forms, tune the base chakra and other powerful work. Build 10 angelic instruments worth $700.

$25.00 Softcover 96p ISBN 0-929385-63-2

PRISONERS OF EARTH

Psychic Possession and Its Release

Aloa Starr

The symptoms, causes and release techniques in a documented exploration by a practitioner. A fascinating study that demystifies possession.

$11.95 Softcover 179p ISBN 0-929385-37-3

✦ RICHARD DANNELLEY

SEDONA POWER SPOT, VORTEX AND MEDICINE WHEEL GUIDE

Discover why this book is so popular! Six detailed maps, special meditations for each power spot, and a lot of heart. Richard Dannelley is a native of the Sedona area.

NEW! SEDONA: BEYOND THE VORTEX

The Ultimate Journey to Your Personal Place of Power

An advanced guide to ascension, using vortex power, sacred geometry, and the Merkaba.

THIS WORLD AND THE NEXT ONE

Aiello

A handbook about your life before birth and your life after death, it explains the how and why of experiences with space people and dimensions. Man in his many forms is a "puppet on the stage of creation."

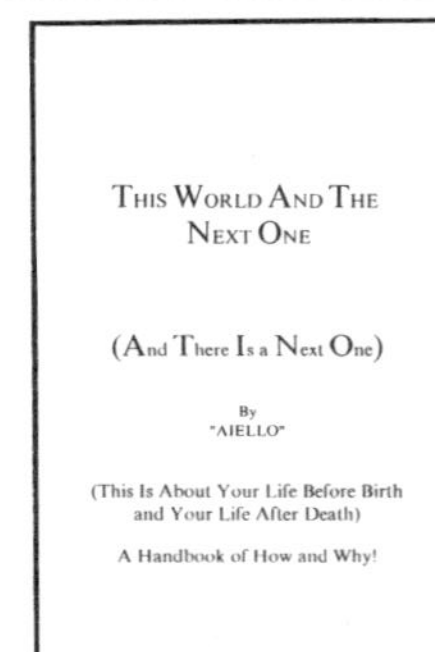

NEW!

MERGING DIMENSIONS

with Linda Bradshaw

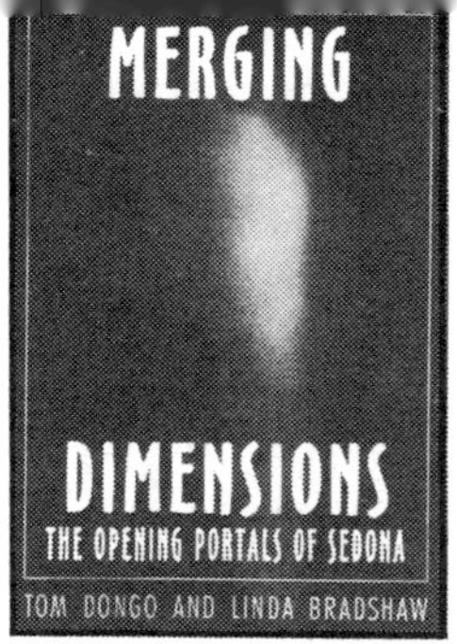

The authors' personal experiences. 132 photographs of strange events, otherworldly beings, strange flying craft, unexplained light anomalies. *They're leaving physical evidence!*

$14.95 Softcover 200p ISBN 0-9622748-4-4

UNSEEN BEINGS UNSEEN WORLDS

Venture into unknown realms with a leading researcher. Discover new information on how to communicate with nonphysical beings, aliens, ghosts, wee people and the Gray zone. Photos of ET activity and interaction with humans.

$9.95 Softcover 122p ISBN 0-9622748-3-6

THE LEGEND OF THE EAGLE CLAN

Cathleen M. Cramer with Derren A. Robb

The emotionally charged story of Morning Glory, a remembrance of her life 144 years ago as part of the Anasazi, the ancient ones. This book is for those who need to remember who they are.

$12.95 Softcover 281p ISBN 0-929385-68-3

THE ALIEN TIDE

The Mysteries of Sedona II

UFO/ET events and paranormal activity in the Sedona area and U.S. are investigated by a leading researcher who cautions against fear of the alien presence. For all who seek new insights. Photos/illustrations.

$7.95 Softcover 128p ISBN 0-9622748-1-X

THE QUEST

The Mysteries of Sedona III

Fascinating in-depth interviews with 26 who have answered the call to Sedona and speak of their spiritual experiences. Explores the mystique of the area and effect the quests have had on individual lives. Photos/illustrations.

$8.95 Softcover 144p ISBN 0-9622748-2-8

THE MYSTERIES OF SEDONA

An overview of the New Age Mecca that is Sedona, Arizona. Topics are the famous energy vortexes, UFOs, channeling, Lemuria, metaphysical and mystical experiences and area paranormal activity. Photos/illustrations.

$6.95 Softcover 84p ISBN 0-9622748-0-1

BOOK MARKET

A reader's guide to the extraordinary books we publish, print and market for your enLightenment.

ORDER NOW!
1-800-450-0985
or Fax 1-800-393-7017
Or use order form at end

VISA · MasterCard

✦ BOOKS by ROYAL PRIEST RESEARCH

PRISM OF LYRA

Traces the inception of the human race back to Lyra, where the original expansion of the duality was begun, to be finally integrated on earth. Fascinating channeled information.

$11.95 Softcover 112p ISBN 0-9631320-0-8

VISITORS FROM WITHIN

Explores the extra-terrestrial contact and abduction phenomenon in a unique and intriguing way. Narrative, precisely focused channeling & firsthand accounts.

$12.95 Softcover 171p ISBN 0-9631320-1-6

PREPARING FOR CONTACT

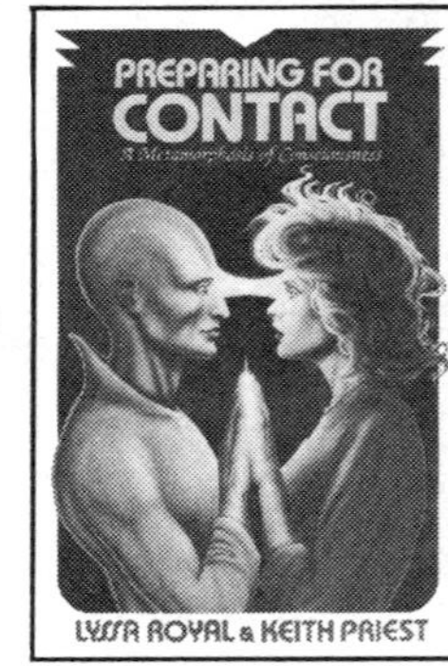

Contact requires a metamorphosis of consciousness, since it involves two species who meet on the next step of evolution. A channeled guidebook to ready us for that transformation. Engrossing.

$12.95 Softcover 188p ISBN 0-9631320-2-4

SOUL RECOVERY & EXTRACTION

Ai Gvhdi Waya

Soul recovery is about regaining the pieces of one's spirit that have been trapped, lost or stolen either by another person or through a traumatic incident that has occurred in one's life.

I'M O.K. I'M JUST MUTATING!

The Golden Star Alliance

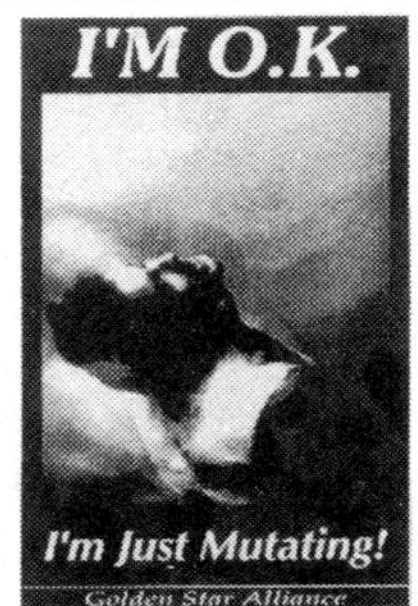

Major shifts are now taking place upon this planet. It is mutating into a Body of Light, as are all the beings who have chosen to be here at this time. A view of what is happening and the mutational symptoms you may

OUR COSMIC ANCESTORS

Maurice Chatelain

A former NASA expert documents evidence left in codes inscribed on ancient monuments pointing to the existence of an advanced prehistoric civilization regularly visited (and technologically assisted) by ETs.

THE MONTAUK PROJECT
Experiments in Time

The truth about time that reads like science fiction! Secret research with invisibility experiments that culminated at Montauk, tapping the powers of creation and manipulating time itself. Exposé by the technical director.

$15.95 Softcover 156p ISBN 0-9631889-0-9

MONTAUK REVISITED
Adventures in Synchronicity

The sequel unmasks the occult forces that were behind the technology of Montauk and the incredible characters associated with it.

$19.95 Softcover 249p ISBN 0-9631889-1-7

PYRAMIDS OF MONTAUK
Explorations in Consciousness

A journey through the mystery schools of Earth unlocking the secret of the Sphinx, thus awakening the consciousness of humanity to its ancient history and origins.

$19.95 Softcover 249p ISBN 0-9631889-2-5

ENCOUNTER IN THE PLEIADES:
An Inside Look at UFOs

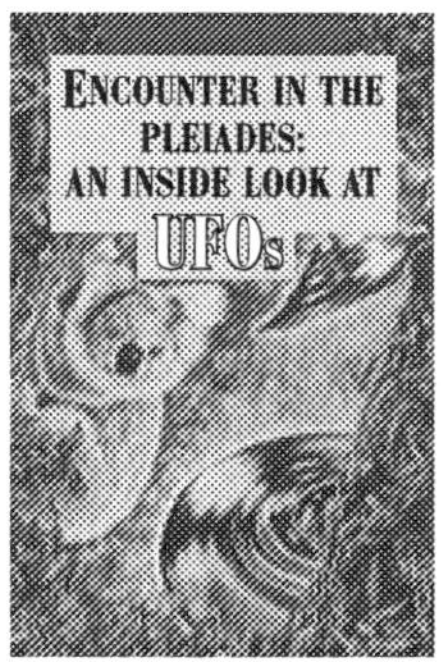

For the first time, the personal history of Preston Nichols is revealed, also amazing information the world has not yet heard. An unprecedented insight into the technology of flying saucers. Never has the complex subject of UFOs been explained in such simple language.

$19.95 Softcover ISBN 0-9631889-3-3

ACCESS YOUR BRAIN'S JOY CENTER
Pete Sanders Jr.

An M.I.T.-trained scientist's discovery of how to self-trigger the brain's natural mood-elevation mechanisms as an alternative to alcohol, nicotine, drugs or overeating to cope with life's pressures and challenges. Combination book and audio cassette package.

$29.95 Softcover 90p plus tape ISBN 0-9641911-0-5

PRINCIPLES TO REMEMBER AND APPLY
Maile

A handbook for the heart and mind, it will spark and expand your remembrance. Explores space, time, relationships, health and includes beautiful meditations and affirmations. Lucid and penetrating.

$11.95 Softcover 114p ISBN 0-929385-59-4

[THE ONLY PLANET] OF CHOICE
Council of Nine through
Phyllis V. Schlemmer

One of the most significant books of our time, updated. About free will and the power of Earth's inhabitants to create a harmonious world. Covers ET civilizations, the nature of the Source of the universe, humanity's ancient history etc.

$14.95 Softcover 342p ISBN 1-85860-023-5

[I]NANNA RETURNS
V.S. Ferguson

A story of the gods and their interaction with humankind. Simple tale by Inanna, whose Pleiadian family, including Enlil and Enki, took over the Earth 500,000 years ago, this story brings the gods to life as real beings with problems and weaknesses, although technologically superior.

$14.00 Softcover 274p

IT'S TIME TO REMEMBER
Joy S. Gilbert

A riveting story of one woman's awakening to alien beings. Joy recounts her initial sightings, dreams and ongoing interaction with nonhuman beings she calls her friends. After her terror, she sees her experiences as transformative and joyful.

$19.95 Hardcover 186p ISBN 0-9645941-4-5

✦ BOOKS by ROBERT SHAPIRO and JULIE RAPKIN

AWAKENING to the ANIMAL KINGDOM

This is channeled from the guiding spirit for various animals. Each animal group has an oversoul who shares new teachings with the animals in that species. Discusses origin, purpose, lifestyle and behavior patterns of various animals.

$8.95 Softcover 86p ISBN 0-945946-02-3

AWAKENING to the PLANT KINGDOM

Stimulating information channeled from the plant kingdom. Plants discuss their universal origins, dreams, procreation, telepathic communication, death and rebirth, connection to the Devic and their preferences for seeding, harvesting and consumption.

$9.95 Softcover 125p ISBN 0-945946-12-0

LIFE ON THE CUTTING EDGE
Sal Rachelle

The most significant questions of our time require a cosmic view of reality. From the evolution of consciousness, dimensions and ETs to the New World Order, this is a no-nonsense book from behind and beyond the scenes. A must-read!

$14.95 Softcover 336p ISBN 0-9640535-0-0

BOOK MARKET

A reader's guide to the extraordinary books we publish, print and market for your enLightenment.

ORDER NOW!
1-800-450-0985
or Fax 1-800-393-7017
Or use order form at end

✦ NEW!

ARCTURUS PROBE
José Argüelles

A poetic depiction of how the Earth was seeded by beings from the Arcturus system of three million years ago. The author of *The Mayan Factor* tells how Atlantis and Elysium were played out on Mars and implanted into Earth consciousness. Illustrated.

$14.95 Softcover ISBN 0-929385-75-6

GUARDIANS OF THE FLAME
Tamar George

Channeled drama of a golden city in a crystal land tells of Atlantis, the source of humanity's ritual, healing, myth and astrology. Life in Atlantis over 12,000 years ago through the eyes of Persephone, a magician who can become invisible. A story you'll get lost in.

$14.95 Softcover ISBN 0-929385-76-4

THE MILLENNIUM TABLETS
John McIntosh

Twelve tablets containing 12 powerful secrets, yet only 2 opened. The Lightbearers and Wayshowers will pave the way, dispelling darkness and allowing the opening of the 10 remaining tablets to humanity, thus beginning the age of total freedom.

$14.95 Softcover ISBN 0-929385-78-0

✦ OLDER CLASSICS

THE TRANSFORMATIVE VISION
José Argüelles

Reprint of his 1975 tour de force, which prophesied the Harmonic Convergence as the "climax of matter," the collapse of materialism. Follows the evolution of the human soul in modern times by reviewing its expressions

OUT-OF-BODY EXPLORATION
Jerry Mulvin

Techniques for traveling in the Soul Body to achieve absolute freedom and experience truth for oneself. Discover reincarnation, karma and your personal spiritual path.

VOICES OF SPIRIT
Charles H. Hapgood

The author discusses 15 years of work with Elwood Babbitt, the famed channel. Will fascinate both the curious sceptic and the believer. Includes complete transcripts.

KRYON – Book I
The End Times

Kryon through
Lee Carroll

New information for personal peace. Valuable metaphysical material presented in a simple easy-to-read manner.

$12.00 Softcover ISBN 0-9636304-2-3

KRYON – Book II
Don't Think Like a Human

Kryon through
Lee Carroll

Channeled answers to basic questions. Leading to a new way of being, which will allowing miracles to come into one's life.

$12.00 Softcover ISBN 0-9636304-0-7

KRYON – Book III
Alchemy of The Human Spirit

Kryon through
Lee Carroll

A guide to human transition into the New Age. Book III of the Kryon books covers predictions, validations, skeptics, science, mathematics and more. Two special appendices on the mysterious 9944 math.

$14.00 Softcover 376p ISBN 0-9636304-8-2

TOUCHED BY LOVE

Dorothy McManus

From the exotic jungles of the Congo to New York's Fifth Avenue, this story sweeps the reader along in a fast-moving adventure of suspense, passion and romance. A strong theme of faith in the Universe is woven throughout the book.

$9.95 Softcover 191p ISBN 0-929686-03-9

POISONS THAT HEAL

Eileen Nauman DHM (UK)

Homeopathy is all that remains to protect us from the deadly superbugs and viruses that modern medicine has failed to turn back. Learn how to protect yourself and your family against the coming Ebola virus and other deadly diseases.

$14.95 Softcover 270p ISBN 0-929385-62-4

PEACE LABYRINTH
Sacred Grometry

Dr. Beatrice Bartnett

The author explains the meaning and significance of the Peace Labyrinth, a sacred geometry space. Using the numerology of the ancient Egyptians, the book explores ways of connecting with God, balancing energy, celebrations and exercises.

$9.95 Softcover 56p ISBN 0-9622182-7-8

BOOK MARKET

A reader's guide to the extraordinary books we publish, print and market for your enLightenment.

ORDER NOW!
1-800-450-0985
or Fax 1-800-393-7017
Or use order form at end

VISA MasterCard

ANNOUNCING a CHILDREN'S DIVISION – STARCHILD PRESS

CACTUS EDDIE

Brian Gold

Imaginative and colorful, charmingly illustrated with 20 detailed paintings by the artist author. The tale of a small boy who when separated from his family has more adventures than Pecos Bill. Printed in large 8½" by 11" format. A beautiful book!

$11.95 Softcover 62p

ISBN 0-929385-74-8

THE GREAT KACHINA

Lou Bader

A warm, delightful story that will help children understand Kachina energy. With 20 full-color illustrations, printed in 8½" by 11" format to dramatize the artwork.

$11.95 Softcover 62p

ISBN 0-929385-60-8

IN THE SHADOW OF THE SAN FRANCISCO PEAKS

Lou Bader

Collection of tales about those who shaped the frontier and were changed by it. A young boy's experiences with people and the wilderness is fascinating reading for all ages.

$9.95 Softcover 152p

ISBN 0-929385-52-7

SPIRIT OF THE NINJA

Toni Siegel

Returning as a dog, a Spiritual Warrior gains love and peace with a young woman in Sedona. Profoundly moving tale for all ages.

SONG OF SIRIUS

Dorothy McManus

A truthful view of modern teens who face drugs and death, love and forgiveness. Guided by Eckrita of Sirius, they each find their destiny and desires.

I WANT TO KNOW

Aloa Starr

Inspiring responses to the questions of Why am I here? Who is God? Who is Jesus? What do dreams mean? and What do angels do? Invites contemplation, sets values and delights the young.

$7.00 Softcover 87p

ISBN 0-929686-02-0

A CIRCLE OF ANGELS
A workbook. An in-depth teaching tool with exercises and illustrations throughout.
$18.95 ISBN 0-929385-87-X

THE 12 UNIVERSAL LAWS
A workbook for all ages. Learning to live the Universal Laws; exercises and illustrations throughout.
$18.95 ISBN 0-929385-81-0

WHERE IS GOD?
Story of a child who finds God in himself and teaches others.
$4.95 ISBN 0-929385-90-X

HAPPY FEET
A child's guide to foot reflexology, with pictures to guide.
$4.95 ISBN 0-929385-88-8

WHEN THE EARTH WAS NEW
Teaches ways to protect and care for our Earth.
$4.95 ISBN 0-929385-91-8

THE ANGEL TOLD ME TO TELL YOU GOODBYE
Near-death experience heals his fear.
$4.95 ISBN 0-929385-84-5

COLOR ME ONE
Lessons in competition, sharing and separateness.
$4.95 ISBN 0-929385-82-9

ONE RED ROSE
Explores discrimination, judgment, and the unity of love.
$4.95 ISBN 0-929385-83-7

WHO'S AFRAID OF THE DARK?
Fearful Freddie learns to overcome with love.
$4.95 ISBN 0-929385-89-6

THE BRIDGE BETWEEN TWO WORLDS
Comfort for the "Star Children" on Earth.
$4.95 ISBN 0-929385-85-3

EXPLORING THE CHAKRAS
Ways to balance energy and feel healthy.
$4.95 ISBN 0-929385-86-1

CRYSTALS FOR KIDS
Workbook to teach care and properties of stones.
$4.95 ISBN 0-929385-92-6

✦ BOOK MARKET ORDER FORM ✦

BOOKS PUBLISHED BY LIGHT TECHNOLOGY PUBLISHING

Title	Author	Price	No. Copies	Total
Acupressure for the Soul	*Fallon*	$11.95	____	$________
Alien Presence	*Ananda*	$19.95	____	$________
Arcturus Probe	*Argüelles*	$14.95	____	$________
Behold a Pale Horse	*Cooper*	$25.00	____	$________
Cactus Eddie	*Gold*	$11.95	____	$________
Channelling	*Vywamus/Burns*	$ 9.95	____	$________
Color Medicine	*Klotsche*	$11.95	____	$________
Explorer Race	*Shapiro*	$25.00	____	$________
Forever Young	*Clark*	$ 9.95	____	$________
Guardians of The Flame	*George*	$14.95	____	$________
Great Kachina	*Bader*	$11.95	____	$________
Legend of the Eagle Clan	*Cramer*	$12.95	____	$________
Living Rainbows	*Bain*	$14.95	____	$________
Mahatma I & II	*Grattan*	$19.95	____	$________
Millennium Tablets	*McIntosh*	$14.95	____	$________
New Age Primer		$11.95	____	$________
Poisons That Heal	*Nauman*	$14.95	____	$________
Prisoners of Earth	*Starr*	$11.95	____	$________
Sedona Vortex Guide Book		$14.95	____	$________
Shadow of San Francisco Peaks	*Bader*	$ 9.95	____	$________
Story of the People	*Rota*	$11.95	____	$________
This World and the Next One	*Aiello*	$ 9.95	____	$________
Light Technology Research/Fanning				
Shining the Light		$12.95	____	$________
Shining the Light – Book II		$14.95	____	$________
Shining the Light – Book III		$14.95	____	$________
Arthur Fanning				
Souls, Evolution & the Father		$12.95	____	$________
Simon		$ 9.95	____	$________
Wesley H. Bateman				
Dragons & Chariots		$ 9.95	____	$________
Knowledge From the Stars		$11.95	____	$________
Lynn Buess				
Children of Light, Children of Denial		$ 8.95	____	$________
Numerology: Nuances in Relationships		$12.65	____	$________
Numerology for the New Age		$ 9.85	____	$________

Title	Price	No. Copies	Total
Ruth Ryden			
The Golden Path	$11.95	____	$________
Living The Golden Path	$11.95	____	$________
Dorothy Roeder			
Crystal Co-Creators	$14.95	____	$________
Next Dimension is Love	$11.95	____	$________
Reach For Us	$14.95	____	$________
Hallie Deering			
Light From the Angels	$15.00	____	$________
Do-It-Yourself Power Tools	$25.00	____	$________
Joshua David Stone, Ph.D.			
Complete Ascension Manual	$14.95	____	$________
Soul Psychology	$14.95	____	$________
Beyond Ascension	$14.95	____	$________
Hidden Mysteries	$14.95	____	$________
Ascended Masters	$14.95	____	$________
Vywamus/Janet McClure			
AHA! The Realization Book	$11.95	____	$________
Light Techniques	$11.95	____	$________
Sanat Kumara	$11.95	____	$________
Scopes of Dimensions	$11.95	____	$________
The Source Adventure	$11.95	____	$________
Evolution: Our Loop of Experiencing	$14.95	____	$________
Leia Stinnett			
A Circle of Angels	$18.95	____	$________
The Twelve Universal Laws	$18.95	____	$________
Where Is God?	$ 4.95	____	$________
Happy Feet	$ 4.95	____	$________
When the Earth Was New	$ 4.95	____	$________
The Angel Told Me To Tell You Goodby	$ 4.95	____	$________
Color Me One	$ 4.95	____	$________
One Red Rose	$ 4.95	____	$________
Exploring the Chakras	$ 4.95	____	$________
Crystals For Kids	$ 4.95	____	$________
Who's Afraid of the Dark	$ 4.95	____	$________
The Bridge Between Two Worlds	$ 4.95	____	$________

BOOKS PRINTED OR MARKETED BY LIGHT TECHNOLOGY PUBLISHING

Title	Author	Price	Qty	Total
Access Your Brain's Joy Center (w/ tape)	*Sanders*	$29.95	____	$________
Awaken to the Healer Within	*Work, Groth*	$ 9.95	____	$________
A Dedication to the Soul/Sole. . .	*Vosacek*	$ 9.95	____	$________
Earth in Ascension	*Clark*	$14.95	____	$________
"I'm OK I'm Just Mutating"	*Golden Star Alliance*	$ 6.00	____	$________
Innana Returns	*Ferguson*	$14.00	____	$________
It's Time To Remember	*Gilbert*	$19.95	____	$________
I Want To Know	*Starr*	$ 7.00	____	$________
Life On the Cutting Edge	*Rachelle*	$14.95	____	$________
Our Cosmic Ancestors	*Chatelain*	$ 9.95	____	$________
Out-Of-Body Exploration	*Mulvin*	$ 8.95	____	$________
Peace Labyrinth	*Bartnett*	$ 9.95	____	$________
Principles To Remember and Apply	*Maile*	$11.95	____	$________
Sedona Starseed	*Mardyks*	$14.95	____	$________
Song of Sirius	*McManus*	$ 8.00	____	$________
Soul recovery and Extraction	*Waya*	$ 9.95	____	$________
Spirit of The Ninja	Siege	$ 7.95	____	$________
Temple of The Living Earth	*Christine*	$16.00	____	$________
The Only Planet of Choice	*Schlemmer*	$14.95	____	$________
Touched By Love	*McManus*	$ 9.95	____	$________
We Are One	*Norquist*	$14.95	____	$________

Title	Price	Qty	Total
Richard Dannelley			
Sedona Power Spot/Guide	$11.00	____	$________
Sedona: Beyond The Vortex	$12.00	____	$________
Tom Dongo: Mysteries of Sedona			
Mysteries of Sedona — Book I	$ 6.95	____	$________
Alien Tide—Book II	$ 7.95	____	$________
Quest—Book III	$ 8.95	____	$________
Unseen Beings, Unseen Worlds	$ 9.95	____	$________
Merging Dimensions	$14.95	____	$________
Preston B. Nichols with Peter Moon			
Montauk Project	$15.95	____	$________
Montauk Revisited	$19.95	____	$________
Pyramids of Montauk	$19.95	____	$________
Encounter in the Pleiades: Inside Look at UFOs	$19.95	____	$________
Lyssa Royal and Keith Priest			
Preparing For Contact	$12.95	____	$________
Prism of Lyra	$11.95	____	$________
Visitors From Within	$12.95	____	$________
Robert Shapiro			
Awakening To The Animal Kingdom	$ 8.95	____	$________
Awakening To The Plant Kingdom	$ 9.95	____	$________

ASCENSION MEDITATION TAPES

Title	Code	Price	Qty	Total
JOSHUA DAVID STONE, PH.D.				
Ascension Activation Meditation	S101	$12.00	____	$________
Tree of Life Ascension Meditation	S102	$12.00	____	$________
Mt. Shasta Ascension Activation Meditation	S103	$12.00	____	$________
Kabbalistic Ascension Activation	S104	$12.00	____	$________
Complete Ascension Manual Meditation	S105	$12.00	____	$________
Set of all 5 tapes		$49.95	____	$________
VYWAMUS/BARBARA BURNS				
The Quantum Mechanical You (6 tapes)	B101-6	$40.00	____	$________

Title	Code	Price	Qty	Total
BRIAN GRATTAN				
Seattle Seminar Resurrection 1994 (12 tapes)	M102	$79.95	____	$________
YHWH/ARTHUR FANNING				
On Becoming	F101	$10.00	____	$________
Healing Meditations/Knowing Self	F102	$10.00	____	$________
Manifestation & Alignment w/ Poles	F103	$10.00	____	$________
The Art of Shutting Up	F104	$10.00	____	$________
Continuity of Consciousness	F105	$25.00	____	$________
Black-Hole Meditation	F106	$10.00	____	$________
Merging the Golden Light Replicas of You	F107	$10.00	____	$________

BOOKSTORE DISCOUNTS HONORED

☐ CHECK ☐ MONEY ORDER

CREDIT CARD: ☐ MC ☐ VISA

____

Exp. date: ____________________

Signature: ____________________

(U.S. FUNDS ONLY) PAYABLE TO:

LIGHT TECHNOLOGY PUBLISHING

P.O. BOX 1526 • SEDONA • AZ 86339
(520) 282-6523 FAX: (520) 282-4130
1-800-450-0985
Fax 1-800-393-7017

NAME/COMPANY ____________________

ADDRESS ____________________

CITY/STATE/ZIP ____________________

PHONE ____________________ CONTACT ____________________

SUBTOTAL: $ __________

SALES TAX: $ __________
(7.5% – AZ residents only)

SHIPPING/HANDLING: $ __________
($3 Min.; 10% of orders over $30)

CANADA S/H: $ __________
(20% of order)

TOTAL AMOUNT ENCLOSED: $ __________

All prices in US$. Higher in Canada and Europe.

CANADA: CHEREV CANADA, INC. 1(800) 263-2408 FAX (519) 986-3103 • ENGLAND/EUROPE: WINDRUSH PRESS LTD. 0608 652012/652025 FAX 0608 652125
AUSTRALIA: GEMCRAFT BOOKS (03)888-0111 FAX (03)888-0044 • NEW ZEALAND: PEACEFUL LIVING PUB. (07)571-8105 FAX (07)571-8513

BOOKSTORE DISCOUNTS HONORED

☐ CHECK ☐ MONEY ORDER

CREDIT CARD: ☐ MC ☐ VISA

____

Exp. date: ____________________

Signature: ____________________

(U.S. FUNDS ONLY) PAYABLE TO:

LIGHT TECHNOLOGY PUBLISHING

P.O. BOX 1526 • SEDONA • AZ 86339
(520) 282-6523 FAX: (520) 282-4130
1-800-450-0985
Fax 1-800-393-7017

NAME/COMPANY ____________________

ADDRESS ____________________

CITY/STATE/ZIP ____________________

PHONE ____________________ CONTACT ____________________

SUBTOTAL: $ __________

SALES TAX: $ __________
(7.5% – AZ residents only)

SHIPPING/HANDLING: $ __________
($3 Min.; 10% of orders over $30)

CANADA S/H: $ __________
(20% of order)

TOTAL AMOUNT ENCLOSED: $ __________

All prices in US$. Higher in Canada and Europe.

CANADA: CHEREV CANADA, INC. 1(800) 263-2408 FAX (519) 986-3103 • ENGLAND/EUROPE: WINDRUSH PRESS LTD. 0608 652012/652025 FAX 0608 652125
AUSTRALIA: GEMCRAFT BOOKS (03)888-0111 FAX (03)888-0044 • NEW ZEALAND: PEACEFUL LIVING PUB. (07)571-8105 FAX (07)571-8513